Wet Socks

Oorjit Sethi

FanatiXx® Publication

FanatiXx® Publication
AM/56, Basanti Colony, Rourkela 769012, Odisha
ISO 9001:2015 Certified

By: Oorjit Sethi
ISBN: 978-93-5605-303-8
Book: Wet Socks
Price: INR 249/-

Printing By: BooksClub.in

DISCLAIMER

Table of Contents

About the Author:

I'm someone who thinks life is both simpler and stranger than people admit. I'm in grade 12, and I've discovered that growing up is mostly just realizing your ideas about everything are under construction permanently.

I like reading things that make me pause, coding things that sometimes break, and joking around just enough that the world feels a little lighter. If there's a serious topic, chances are I'll find a way to slip in a dumb observation about it, mostly because taking yourself too seriously is an excellent way to miss the point.

I've written fiction, I've abandoned fiction, and now I mostly collect thoughts that don't fit neatly anywhere else. Some are curious, some are a little ridiculous, and all of them are a mixture of mine and things I've read on the Internet. Comic books and superhero movies are a huge inspiration: you have no idea the amount of things you can learn from Spider-Man. Not science or math, nothing tangible, but definitely abilities which will make you a good person, which is really the most important part.

Most of the time, I'm just trying to make sense of why people act the way they do, why the internet behaves like an organism with its own moods, and why optimism feels like such a complicated sport.

If you're here, you're basically stepping into the same puddle I keep stepping into: except this time, it's on purpose. Welcome to my Wet Socks.

Foreword by Mr M M Murugappan

When I first read Oorjit Sethi's compilation of Drips, Wet Socks, I was awestruck. It was a perfect example of a quotation by Neil Blumenthal, "Creativity flows when Curiosity is Stoked".

Oorjit is my friend. We are more than fifty years apart in age, our conversations often in the sylvan surroundings of his family home in Indore, India meander into a vast variety of subjects from world history and geopolitics to interests of current day youth and how they traverse the use technology and media. He will soon graduate from high school and will go an institution of higher learning. However, my learnings from him are immense, especially from his world view, versatility of thought, and, profundity of knowledge that spans science, sport and society with equal ease,

Wet Socks is unique in many ways. It is not just about the authors' experiences and insights on many subjects. It draws the reader into a domain that requires reflection and introspection across many topics which will kindle deep thought beyond just casual interest. Its variety drew me into a realm of reality or at times fantasy and gave me to understand the fact that age does not necessarily give rise to progressive wisdom. It has caused much inquiry within me and has changed my thoughts on many subjects. For this I am indeed grateful to the author.

Oorjit has marked his favorite Drips. His readers will mark theirs. My favorite however is the one captioned "Destiny". In this Oorjit discusses the topic in a manner that we have all experienced and, finally, concludes that faith in destiny and hope may be one and the same, both being driven by a vision of a better future, and both requiring commitment to making that vision a reality.

Salutations for creating and sharing "Wet Socks" with the world. May your stars Oorjit and those of your readers continue to rise always, as you inspire minds, question seemingly time-tested narratives and above all help us be better people.

Wet Socks is a must read for everyone, across all ages.

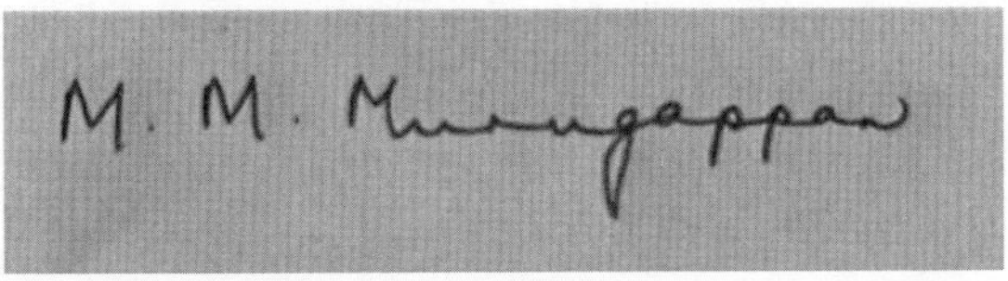

Mr. M. M. Murugappan
Former Chairman, Murugappa Group, India

Introduction/Prologue

There is a very particular sort of unease that arises from jumping in a puddle with the water wetting not just your shoes, but seeping into your socks. It's not uncomfortable — it's just persistently annoying. Your whole day is now a little wet, a little annoying, a little more real than you'd like it to be. That's sort of what it feels like to grow up. An endless blend of grandiose ideas and petty irritations, epiphanies that strike at inconvenient moments, and questions that remain in your mind far too long.

That's Wet Socks. A bunch of thoughts that I like to call drips—sometimes profound, sometimes stupid, sometimes somewhere in the middle—seen through my eyes: a teenager making sense of the world. These are not refined theories. They're thoughts I jotted down because they refused to leave me alone.

And that’s the thing about being a teenager: your mind wanders. It doesn’t shut up.

Some days I’m wondering about optimism and why it seems more difficult than it appears. Other days I’m questioning why people lie or if we’re actually free to make choices. Either I’m ranting about how the internet plays games with our minds, or how people will despise something just because it’s trendy. Other times I just need to ramble about YouTube, or wonder if time travel should even be allowed.

The subjects here are everywhere — but so is teen life. You can flip from worrying about the future to freaking out about the past, to giggling at a meme, to questioning whether AI will ultimately destroy everything… all within the same afternoon.

These thoughts leave me damp, like wet socks. Even after they dry up, you still end up thinking about that feeling.

I suppose what I’m attempting to convey is: life does not slow down for you to take notes. You’re meant to learn from experience, but half the time you don’t even know you had an experience until three days later when you’re in the shower and suddenly it all makes sense. Or doesn’t. Either way, that’s how most of these entries originate.

Before I landed on this, I used to write fiction. Two entire books, to be specific — when I was 12 and 13. Like every 12-year old’s mind, the books were completely unfiltered and absolutely overflowing with imagination. At that age you just feel like Disneyland had spread its roots through the whole world. Imagination was purer back then. Ideas came in waves I was just waiting to surf on, and plotlines were weaved with bliss.

Then came the inevitable phase people like to call growing up. Now, it is hard to imagine something as jolly as those times when my world was a series of storybooks and YouTube Gameplays. My mind became thicker, more complex. Midway through my third book I began to notice the gaps in the storyline: Arcs that never quite finished, threads that were never quite connected. It's still somewhere in the cloud, a half-finished monument to what happens when imagination is let loose.

Sometime after that, I stopped trying to make something from a whole lot of nothing. I quit trying to create a utopian world and began chronicling the strange, unreliable one in my mind. The actual one. That's when the words finally felt right. That's when Wet Socks started.

So, this is my playlist of drips. Some are tiny drops; some are gushes of consciousness. All of them are mine.

Press plays wherever you like — and feel free to step into my discomfort zone: my Wet Socks.

You are Who you Pretend to Be*

- May 29, 2025

Let's talk about identity. Not in the abstract or theoretical way but in the real, everyday kind of way. The who are you when you're half-asleep while doom scrolling. kind of way.

You probably think you know who you are. You've got a name, an about on social media, a music playlist that describes you better than words ever could. But pause for a second. If you were to take away every visible signal, like the likes, the comments, the tags, the profile pictures, what would be left? And would that version of you still feel like you?

The thing is, we are all actors. I don't mean fake, but more like filtered. You act differently in front of your parents than you do with your friends. You use a different kind of speech in a job interview compared to on Snapchat. And on texts you're probably a curated, refined version of yourself.

So, the question isn't "Are you being fake?" It's "Which version of you are you being today?"

This isn't a digital crisis caused by the rise of social media like what people say is the cause of every other problem. It's a human truth that's just amplified now. In the past, your identity was largely shaped by geography, family, and culture. Now, it's also shaped by your internet history, your DMs, your subreddits. You might live in the US, but your soul lives on a forum with hundreds of strangers who understand your exact niche.

And here's the paradox. We're told to be ourselves, but also told to build a personal brand. We're told to be authentic, but also to remember that employers might see our tweets. So we start mixing truth with strategy. We fillet away edges. We try on masks, and some don't fit, some surprise us, and some we keep for the rest of the ride.

Is that wrong?

Maybe identity was never supposed to be a fixed thing. Maybe the pressure to be one consistent person is actually what's unnatural. Let's think about it. Every major phase of your life had a different you. You were a different person at 12 than you are now, and thank God for that. You'll probably enjoy talking about property values when you're older. So why is digital identity, the version of us that is allowed the most space to experiment, expected to stay the same?

Maybe pretending is actually practice.

Maybe the version of yourself you perform today online is a sketch of who you're trying to become, who you want to be. You post confident things when you're scared. You try humor when you feel awkward. You say smart things to believe them yourself. That's not fake. That's growth.

So maybe you aren't who you pretend to be. Maybe:

You Will Be Who You Pretend to Be*

#Drip02

We Need To Adapt

- May 02, 2025

So, you're at some family function, and a relative begins complaining about how "kids these days need to go touch grass" or how “world hunger could be eliminated with the end of social media." You just smile and nod, because what else can you do? But inside you know better. The world is evolving, whether you like it or not.

However, adapting is not about disrespecting tradition. It's about understanding that if we don’t accept what’s coming, we’ll be left behind. Just like how farming was reinvented after the industrial revolution, or how the printing press transformed the way information was delivered, we're in the midst of another change.

Take MrBeast. At a glance, he's a YouTuber giving out money in theatrics on videos. Turn that glance into a gaze though, and he's digging wells in Africa, planting millions of trees, and doing what international aid organizations speak about but cannot achieve. He's not an anomaly. He's among a new crop of digital philanthropists who know how attention works and apply that power to create real change. But there are still individuals who dismiss him because "he just makes YouTube videos." That is the issue. The inability to evolve blinds people to new methods of value.

Speaking of jobs, those same individuals who complain about unemployment also claim that gaming or vlogging doesn't count as work. But reality says something different: streaming isn't hitting a button and screaming at a screen. Creators spend hours editing, writing, promoting, interacting with their community, and learning the platforms they're on. A 9-to-5 where the office is your bedroom and the work never actually ends. Kai Cenat once did a 30-day nonstop marathon. I'm sure that keeping hundreds of thousands of people entertained for 30 days straight is not something anyone can do. The work ethic is genuine. The skills are genuine. The money? Very genuine.

The reality is, to adapt doesn't necessarily mean to agree with all. It means to be willing to learn. You may not wish to open a Twitch channel, and that's okay. But don't discredit the thousands who are earning a living off of one. You may not understand why someone would sit and watch someone else play Minecraft for hours. But guess what? Millions do. And it brings people joy. Isn't that sort of the point? Don't actors and directors essentially do the same thing with movies?

It's easy to remain mired in the past. It's comfortable. But change never happened because of comfort. It happened because of people who experimented with new things, failed, tried again, and persevered. Even when it was easy to just keep holding onto what was.

The truth is, the world's not slowing down. And the more we try to move in the opposite direction, the more we fall behind. Adaptation is no longer a choice, but a necessity. It's how you remain relevant, how you grow, and how you make a real dent in a world that doesn't stop moving.

#Drip03

Are you you?

- May 20, 2025

So, you aced a test. Well done! But let's take a step back. Was it really you who aced it, or was it everything that has ever shaped you into becoming who you are today, from parents, teachers, friends, to even the rock you kick while on the way to school?

This is the modern spin on the Ship of Theseus question. If every part of a newborn is slowly swapped out and shaped by their environment over time, do they still count as themselves? Or are they more like a google doc of a person, constantly edited by everything around them?

Everybody loves giving credit to a specific person. Self-made success stories, personal growth arcs, character over circumstance. But that's only half the truth. The environment is more than just noise. It is responsible for, well, you. The way your brain has wired itself and continues to do so has been shaped by your parents' tone of voice, the way your school runs, everything. You don't exist in a vacuum. You can't exist in a vacuum.

Everybody loves blaming a specific person as well. As humanity, what do we love more than pointing fingers? Can you really blame a person who turned out to be a thief when their whole family is known for burglary?

However, it's not fair to say you're just a product of your surroundings either. Identical twins can be as different as anyone, even when raised in the same household, going to the same school. Choice still exists. You are a canvas and one of a thousand painters. You are the sum of a billion external brushstrokes, a majority of them yours.

So, when you succeed, yes, part of it is you grinding and pushing. But a good part of you is the sum of your best friend who encouraged you, the YouTube video you saw, or the ID card that stopped working.

It's not about blaming the environment or glorifying the individual. It's about understanding that every win, every loss, every moment you experience is built on a scaffolding of experience, people, time, and chance.

So, is it the world that built you, or is it the moments where you rose above just your environment, above what your surroundings wanted you to be, and became the actual, real you?

The Human Need for God

- March 16, 2024

The earliest mention of God in history is a piece of rock, which dates back to 840 BCE (crazy, right?). The inscriptions on the rock refer to the Israeli god Yahweh.

840 BCE was a long, long time ago. What brought about the need for humans to even desire a deity that they consensually agreed was above them? Superior to them? It's common knowledge that us Homo sapiens consider ourselves the 'top dog'. The end of the food chain. So, what series of events might have led us to believe in, or invent, something that was fundamentally better than us?

The earth has been plagued by natural disasters ever since it was formed. Earlier humans could not explain it. They did not have concepts of warm or moist air, or updrafts, or anything of the sort. With a brain like ours, we strive to explain anything and everything. Something like a tornado, which seemed like dark magic? No human could do that. It had to be a being who surpasses a Homosapien. That is God.

This is just one example of circumstances leading to a belief in God.

It's raining when I need to go to school? It's raining. God clearly doesn't want me to go outside.

A new vaccine was made? It's not natural. God did not make it. God wouldn't want me to take it.

That person doesn't believe in God? God wouldn't want him to have a good life. I'll ruin it.

In the above examples, God is just being used to justify what a person wants to do. God could easily be substituted by personal choices.

I hate getting wet, so I will not go in the rain.

I'm scared of needles, so I do not really want to take a vaccine.

That person is not like me, so I will discriminate against him.

People may do what they think is 'right' because that is what God would've done. God is always right.

Now let's take a step back for a second. What is 'right'? Is it right to steal money? Most people will go with a definite no. Is it right to report a plagiarizing colleague who can barely make ends meet? This is where the line starts to blur, where people become unsure what 'right' is.

In my opinion, the 'right' choice for humans depends on the time period and the generation. 4 or 5 generations ago, same-sex marriage was not 'right'. Now? You say this there will be 10 hashtags made against you on Twitter (X).

Nowadays it's deemed okay to fight in the UFC. After a couple generations it may be illegal.

This is where God comes in. Since 840 BCE, God has existed in one way or another. So many things have changed, but not the conviction that a higher power exists. God is constant. Which is why God can act as a North Star. The path which is 'right'. Obama's opinion may not be set in stone, but God's opinion literally is. This is the true need for God. To show us the difference between right and wrong. To be humanity's guide in the vast and blurry plain of moral and ethical choices. To be a cicerone for eternity.

#Drip5

Why People Lie

\- March 19, 2025

Lying. A skill as old as humanity itself. Think about it—when was the first time you lied? Probably when you were a kid, caught red-handed with a cookie in your hand after being told it needed protection from your everlasting hunger. “I found them like this,” you whispered, the crumbs betraying you.

But why do we feel like we need to bend the truth? The answer isn’t as straightforward as “sometimes people are bad.” Lying is something our ancestors used to survive, and something the present generations use as a social lubricant.

It’s hardwired into our brains. Cavemen relied on deceptions and fake emotions to outmaneuver predators and gain advantages over rivals. Even today, you see it in the animal kingdom—a chameleon’s camouflage, a parrot’s mimicry, and swallows' fake distress calls are all nature's way of lying. Humans just evolved to take it to another level. A job interview? You're extremely passionate about spreadsheets.

If lying's really so bad, let's imagine a world without lying. A world where every person was brutally honest. No sugarcoating, no white lies. Your friend asks, "How do I look in this outfit?" and instead of a usual, "You look great!" you respond with, "Did you find those clothes in 1987?" Human interaction would take a turn for the worse, with people have their feelings hurt left, right, and center. Lies keep things running smoothly. They help us navigate social situations without bumping into an obstacle. It's not always malicious—sometimes, it's just the price of getting along with people.

Then there are the lies of self-defense. The ones told to escape trouble, dodge blame, or maintain dignity. "The WiFi wasn't working, that's why I didn't reply." "I didn't see your text." "I totally read the terms and conditions." Lies like these are tiny shields, protecting us from embarrassment, punishment, or just awkward conversations. These lies are not good, but what do we have if not our pride?

Not all lies are innocent. Some are weapons. Some are tools for control. History is littered with grand deceptions—politicians spinning narratives, corporations hiding scandals, dictators rewriting history. When the truth is inconvenient, a well-crafted lie is often the easier alternative.

Despite its usefulness, lying comes with a price. A web of lies is just that—a web. The more you make, the harder it becomes to break free. You get trapped in it. Lies are high maintenance. Forget one, and everything crumbles. And when it's exposed, trust is shattered. People don't remember the "why" behind the lie, just that they were deceived.

The biggest irony? People lie to avoid consequences, but often, the lie itself leads to even worse consequences. A bad decision can be forgiven. A lie? Not so much.

Optimism

\- March 27, 2025

There are two types of people in the world: the ones who see a problem and think, Well, that's it. We're doomed, and the ones who see the same problem and say, alright, let's figure this out. The difference between them? Optimism. It's not something fluffy that individuals just adopt in order to feel good about themselves—it's an underlying way of looking at the world, one that actually affects how we react to whatever life throws at us. Most importantly, it's the distinction between individuals who create things, and those who allow things to happen to them.

Some people think about optimism and automatically dismiss it as having your head in the clouds. That it's not realistic. But true optimism isn't about pretending the world is fine when it's not. It's about examining a situation, looking at it honestly, and trusting that even when it is terrible, even when it is not fair, even when it is impossible to resolve, there is nonetheless a way out. It's not blind positivity; it's not giving up on letting negativity be the answer.

That refusal to give up is what differentiates people. Optimism powers resilience. When a pessimist fails, they look at evidence that they weren't good enough, that their ideas were stupid, that attempting was a waste of time to start with. An optimist looks at the same failure and says, Okay, that didn't work. What do they do next? They don't let failure stop them—they utilize it. They learn from it. They move on, because hope still exists.

And the thing is—optimism really works. Why? Because what you anticipate from life has an impact on how you experience it. If you think things are going to go wrong, you unconsciously put less effort in. Why try? You hold back. But if you think there is a chance of success, you try harder. You fight longer. You take the odds, whatever they may be. Optimistic people don't deny reality—they create it.

Life won't always work out as intended, of course. Occasionally, things will go awry. Optimism doesn't prevent bad things from occurring, but pessimism doesn't as well. All that negativity does is cause you to feel defeated before you even try to do it.

Therefore, when forced to choose between expecting the worst and hoping for something better, optimism is always the better wager. It's not being unrealistic. It's seeing that in every failure, in every setback, in every instance of doubt, there is always a possibility—a possibility worth pursuing. And those who pursue it? They're the ones who make everything different.

#Drip7

The Problem with The Internet

\- February 28, 2025

In the digital era, the world online is now becoming what seems to be a culture of animosity—where everyone is a glass half empty kinda person. Relentless hate has been known to often drown out people trying to voice their appreciation and meaningful debates. The shift has manifested on a wide range of platforms, from social networks to forums, impacting public figures as well as everyday individuals.

There used to be a time when society eagerly celebrated its icons, drawing inspiration from their accomplishments. A world where ESPN analysts are passionate about the sport and not the controversy that drives engagement. Today, however, the story has shifted toward fault-finding rather than praise. Take NBA legend, LeBron James, whose extraordinary skills and contributions to basketball are frequently met with unwarranted hostility online. Everywhere you see he is being put down, whether through his age, his stats, or even his own son. Veteran coach Doc Rivers has noted, "Back in my day, we used to celebrate our stars." It should be embarrassing for the entire NBA community that a person has had to even say this.

These days, social media platforms tend to be home to echo chambers—the algorithm thinks you agree with a specific viewpoint, and so it shows you more of it so you will be pleased by the app. Within these so-called safe spaces, hate grows faster than you can say stop. And the way Reddit works, the more people disagree with you, the farther down the feed your comment goes.

While the surge in online hostility is disheartening and definitely overwhelming, it is important to remember that criticism, when offered with good intentions, is essential for accountability and improvement. An example that comes to mind is tech YouTuber, Marques Brownlee. In late 2024, he encountered significant backlash after sharing a sponsored video in which he was seen driving at 95 mph in a 35-mph zone—a dangerous lapse that drew widespread reproach. People trusted this guy to tell them which cars are good and which aren't, and now he was seen abusing one?

In response, Marques publicly acknowledged his error, calling his actions "absolutely inexcusable and dangerous."

Similarly, his "Panels" app, which had faced criticism for its steep subscription fees and intrusive ads, was overhauled based on user feedback, demonstrating how well-founded critique can lead to meaningful and useful improvements.

The key challenge lies within differentiating between pointing out a mistake to ameliorate the situation and hating because you have nothing better to do.

#Drip8

The AI and Corporate Dilemma

- February 18, 2025

Mega corporations and companies are not your friends. They are not there to help you through tough times. They are emotionless, logical machinations designed for one thing: making money. Securing the bag. Hearing the Ka-Ching. Whether it's selling pizzas, computers, or automated cars, the goal is always to maximize profit, minimize cost, and hope that the consumer becomes the product. This is the reality of the world we live in, and AI is just the latest cog in the relentless race for efficiency.

And it should be no different. Darwin said it the best. People who adapt, survive, those who don't… get laid off. We all wish we lived in a world like "Three Idiots". All of us saw Virus as the villain. I think he was just being realistic. "Life is a race. If you're not at the front of the pack, you'll be left behind sooner or later."

So, when companies lay off 9-5 workers in favor of those who can work 24/7 without a break, is it cruel? Yes, definitely. Is it unfortunate? Sure. But is it wrong? That depends on how you define "wrong." If a business's aim is to survive in a competitive market, then the utmost efficiency is crucial.

Throughout history, new technology has always displaced workers. The Industrial Revolution put millions of craftsmen out of business. The internet eliminated entire industries. And now, AI is doing what AI was built to do—work faster, cheaper, and without so much as a breather between work. But blaming corporations for this shift is like blaming texts for putting carrier pigeons out of a job. Innovation doesn't wait for anyone.

If AI can handle customer service, write software, or design graphics better, faster, and cheaper than a human employee, why wouldn't a company want to make the switch? They aren't charity organizations. Not adapting to better technologies will result in them being left in the wake of their competitors.

AI has not resulted in the system being broken. It has made the system evolve.

Crack

- February 10, 2025

Basketball is a fun game, right? To watch and to play. However, injuries are a buzzkill. They allowed the Indiana Pacers to reach the Conference Finals, and they also stopped my momentum dead in its tracks, right before the most important exam I could take in my school years.

Countless past papers could not have prepared me for what lay ahead: the scribe situation.

I could not write my own paper. Confidence rushed my brain still, thinking, “I could just tell him what to write and he’ll write it. This is better than writing on my own!”

I have never been more wrong in my life.

Dictating your thoughts for someone else to write them down, especially in a math paper, felt like playing a video game but with a 2 second lag. Imagine your player is getting shot at and he moves a year after he is shot. This is what that felt like.

The second shot to the chest was the sudden plunge my typing speed took. I have poured several hundred hours into it, but after the fracture, it dropped from a glorious 122 WPM to a depressing 65. Now, even while I am typing this, the countless errors and the extra time it took for me to write this out, breaks my heart, along with my finger.

#Drip10

Our Longing for The Past

- January 11, 2025

Hindsight is a gift not many people have. It allows us to learn from our mistakes and maybe, hopefully, do better moving forward, whatever that may be.

However, hindsight has a way of pulling us in. Making us stay with it rather than move past it. “What I could’ve done” is a question that haunts every single human being. Our present is washed away with thoughts of the past, and the future is barely given a second thought until it turns into ‘what was’. This is an endless loop of regret, and being unable to let go of the anchor buried deep within the beaches of the last island is what makes many people drown.

The widespread influence of this pandemic is obvious throughout history. Take the NBA, for example. When Michael Jordan was having his dominant reign over the league, everyone was saying the same thing: “Kareem was better”. Kareem’s peak was somewhere in the 1970s, and every old head was leaning towards him in the GOAT debate. Fast forward to 2025, where LeBron James has had the league in a choke hold for 22 years, and everyone is saying the same thing: “Jordan was better”.

The trend shows that around 20-30 years from now, another player will be put up against LeBron, and will face the same thing he did. "Bron was better".

Keeping in touch with the past in the sense of nostalgia is helpful. It reminds us of good times, or bad times, and in some cases give us a much-needed brick wall in the cyclone that is life.

Grabbing on to the past and refusing to let go in the sense of not moving forward in life is an ignorant way to live. It blinds us from seeing what is coming and only putting in focus what once was. It's like driving but with only the rear-view mirror. Can't make much sense of whether to turn right or left, can you? And sooner or later, you will crash. It's completely up to you whether you want to start looking ahead to save your life or keep looking back, refusing to acknowledge how stupidly you are driving your car.

What Beast Games Means for The Future of YouTube

- December 24, 2024

The game show made by MrBeast in collaboration with Prime Video is breaking records left and right, becoming the most-viewed show on the platform in over 82 countries. Insane numbers, especially for a YouTuber. I mean, it wasn't even considered a "job" until 7 or 8 years ago. It's a great achievement for MrBeast and other YouTubers as well; they are taken a lot more seriously by the whole world now, and a large portion of that credit does go to MrBeast.

Jimmy Donaldson has also pioneered what we call "production-heavy videos" in the modern era of YouTube. His budgets have exceeded a million dollars per video several times now, which is great, but it does take away from what YouTube was made for in the first place: bridging the gap between audiences and creators, one that is a chasm in Hollywood.

Let's rewind a bit. MrBeast built this empire on YouTube with ideas like spending 24 hours on top of a mountain or buried alive. It was content that felt fresh (ironically), personal, and a little crazy. But as his projects grew in scale—multi-million-dollar budgets, MCU-level editing, and Hollywood-level stunts—it started setting a new bar on the platform. Now, content creators feel like they have to do the same thing. They have to take up large scale videos, otherwise they will fall to every creator's worst nightmare: fading into irrelevance.

Add these huge, scripted videos into the pot that is YouTube, mix some subscription service into it, and you have… Netflix all over again?

What made YouTube different from other things in the first place? It wasn't polished. It wasn't perfect. It was a place where a person could connect with their viewers. Where viewers could feel that, yeah, this screen is the only thing keeping me from grabbing out and touching them.

Even MrBeast himself is shifting. The guy who once did crazy yet extremely entertaining videos for fun now feels more like a machine churning out content to chase records. Sure, the video is entertaining, but it's hard to not notice that the genuine, personal feeling that drew people to his channel in the first place is taking a backseat. And this isn't just a "MrBeast problem." It is a platform-wide issue. Success on the platform is increasingly defined by how much money you can pour into your videos; not how funny you are or how creatively you can play Minecraft.

#Drip12

There is More to Monsters in Fiction than it Seems

\- December 15, 2024

Those hairy beasts we see so often in movies are definitely an obstacle to overcome for the hero, whether it be to save a princess from a turtle with spikes or get a shiny gem being guarded by a 3 headed dog. But if we take a closer look, these monsters can be utilized for much more than just acting as hurdles for protagonists to overcome. Those creatures that are covered in fur, or have extremely sharp teeth, can always teach us something if we're willing to take the time to hold a mirror out in front of us.

I think we can all agree that Bowser was a wicked person. He looked like a beast from the outside, and he was a psychopath inside. No plot twist there. But any flaw that has ever existed in a character has always been taken from an actual flaw from an actual human. If we can identify what's wrong with Bowser, maybe we could identify what's wrong with us. What we are doing wrong. Of course, it's easier said than done. The turtle had his flaws accentuated so that kids could understand that, "Oh! He's the bad guy!" Humans are usually much more guarded with the way they express their emotions; just ask a teenager. But a minor similarity can still be noticed. Maybe I should try not kidnapping people?

And then there are those monsters that society has shaped and not their own minds and desires.

Take the movie "The Bad Guys". The wolf, the crocodile, or the snake were robbers (and really skilled ones at that), but when their motivations were revealed on later in the movie, everybody who has seen it understood just why they took up this life of crime. It was incredibly strenuous for a wolf to get a job in HR compared to a cute and cuddly animal such as a bunny. However, in the end, these guys turned a new a leaf and become "The Good Guys". An extremely basic and simple redemption arc. Something every human has seen a thousand times. But there's more to it than just being happy the snake got to have a white-collar job.

Monsters in movies like this explain how the world is a lot more morally grey than it appears. Not every robber is a product of the desire for riches. Not every wolf is there to huff and puff and blow the house down.

#Drip13

Everyone is an Expert

- December 02, 2024

From your neighbor to your long-lost relative who only calls to ask your grades, everyone knows just about everything these days. Oh, you got a fracture? Put lotion and some leaves on it and it will be healed… right?

Instagram reels has everyone educated to the point where a PhD is basically useless. However, I don't think people understand just how dangerous it could become in the long run.

More and more people are genuinely starting to believe this stuff. Why go to a doctor when a 22-year-old influencer with no medical degree has a 22 second clip promising to fix your arthritis with flowers torn from the neighbor's dog-poop-infested garden? Suddenly, science-backed medicine looks like the bad guy for not treating you fast enough.

And let's talk about the irony—everyone is ready to put their lives on the line for this faster than life remedy. You slap some mystery herbs on your skin to cure a rash and end up in the ER because it turns out you're allergic to nature itself. The line between quirky life advice and dangerous misinformation is blurrier than ever.

This can lead to some serious problems in the future. Someone could be influenced to take a medication that could cause more harm than actually cure the problem they're facing. Influencers couldn't care less about this. They are getting their views; they are getting publicity. After all, all publicity is good publicity.

Determinism vs Free Will

- November 17, 2024

You - reading this right now. Are you on your device because someone told you to? Because it is secretly written behind a red curtain? Or is it due to your own choice, that you wanted to? I will be trying to dissect this dilemma today, allowing you to choose which one you want to believe.

Determinism is the point of view that yes, everything is decided by some other factor and not you. Whatever you do. Want to eat pizza today? Well, the way you have been brought up, your taste palette, the weather, that birthday party with the burger incident, all of these add up to ultimately making the choice for you: Pizza for dinner sounds amazing. You couldn't possibly make any other choice, because your neurons are going to fire a certain way. Not because you wanted to, but because your past and your present circumstances forced you to, under the guise of "You know what? I don't live with my parents anymore, if I want to eat pizza today, that's what I am going to do.".

On the other hand, free will—the belief that you, as an individual, are capable of making choices independently of outside influences- seems just as plausible. It simplifies everything. Only you decide. Nobody, or nothing, else. It's the idea that you could, at any moment, choose something entirely unexpected—not because of a predetermined chain of events, but simply because you wanted to.

Let's go back to the pizza example. According to free will, you're not eating pizza because your past experiences or your taste buds made the decision for you. You're eating pizza because you sat down, considered your options, and decided that it was what you wanted at that moment. Free will tells you that you can go against the grain. You could choose sushi, even if pizza is your favorite, just to do something different. The choice, free will says, is entirely yours.

Hating on What's Popular

- November 01, 2024

Hating on music that is very popular in the world is really really common. Scorning artists like Drake, Taylor Swift, Sabrina Carpenter, Morgan Wallen, Adele, Billie Eilish, Maroon 5, One Direction, The Weekend, is so quotidian now that it in itself has become mainstream.

Yet so many people listen to them. Drake is raking in 41 million+ streams daily, Taylor Swift is accumulating 64 million streams every day and is on track to overtake Drake as the most streamed artist of all time. So clearly people are listening to these terrible, art-destroying, world-ending, glass-shattering artists.

Numbers don't lie.

People do.

The numbers show that the 200 decibels loud hate these mainstream artists get is just noise. People bash them from the outside, but secretly? They're pressing play. The music's good. That's why so many people love it. So why do humans do this?

Humans have a habit for rooting for the underdog. Always. No one ever roots for the king; they always root for the poor man who is about to kill the king and take the throne. As soon as the poor man has sat on the throne for 8 seconds, people start hating him. And why wouldn't they? It always makes for a nice thrill when encouraging the person who has nothing and is going for everything. Cinderella, Oliver Twist, Aladdin. Stories everyone adores and admires and cherishes.

However, if Cinderella had a nice, loving family, the tale would be… quite stale.

So, when Drake was on the rise in 2011, recently signed by Lil Wayne, releasing his magnum opus, Take Care, everything was sunshine and rainbows. Everybody loved it. Then he released Nothing Was the Same. Still, everyone loved it. IYRTITL was released 2 years later, and it was deemed as an instant classic. Views a year later, and that album broke records. One Dance was being sung by every person you met on the street. Hotline Bling had turned into a viral meme. Everyone knew Drake, and everyone loved Drake. "He's finally done it! One of the greatest rappers of our generation!"

The poor man had finally taken the throne.

After his 8 seconds, the king released More Life.

"Drake fell off."

"Drake is a pop star."

"Drake makes music for girls."

A year later, he finds himself in a feud with a smaller rapper, Push. Guess whose side everyone takes?

Drake loses the rap battle, and people are clowning him all around the world. His fans feel betrayed, his haters have found their new favorite artist in Push, and it just seems like it's over for the man.

Quite literally a month later, Drake releases Scorpion, his new album. It set the record for most streams in a 24-hour period by an album ever. The record was broken in 2021 by — surprise surprise — Drake himself.

The hate and numbers just can't seem to agree.

Whenever someone is on the climb, everyone cheers them on. Because it's exciting.

"I could be that guy. I could be the guy on the rise."

Because people see themselves in those underdogs. They could literally be the guy on the rise. Humans in general can relate more to the little guy. The little guy is one of the people. But when one person makes it to the top but the rest of us are still stuck down here? Can we feel happy for the king?

Destiny

- October 20, 2024

Destiny. Fate. Whatever you want to call it. The notion that everything that might happen to an entity is predetermined. People have been known to give their life to this concept, with the faith that whatever destiny has in store for them, will happen, no matter what. So why try? If the future is already written, why should I make an effort to build it? This kind of mentality is extremely, extremely dangerous, which is why it is necessary to clarify what destiny means for me.

If we take the most common interpretation of it, destiny is what is behind an invisible and intangible curtain. It is a piece of paper that stretches all the way from our conception to our eventual demise. On the paper is written everything that has happened and everything that will.

Everything that has happened is already in your mind, as memories, and whatever will happen is constantly entering your mind, again, as memories. These remembrances-to-come are not known to you until they have already happened.

However, if you could somehow take a peek behind that incorporeal curtain, you'd get those "memories" before they ever happened. But these things that will happen, would they be like reading a book, or like remembering something that hasn't even happened yet, due to the immaterial nature of the actual paper on which your fate is written?

But what happens if we consider destiny to be this solid, locked in place rock? No matter what, it happens. You see the future, and you know the future takes place, since destiny can't mutate.

This is what causes people to become complacent. "Destiny'll take care of it for me."

If you end up in some trouble, "This was supposed to happen, for some reason whatsoever. I'll get out of it, I have faith." This naive faith will be a person's demise. Believing that you will definitely end up in a good place is not a bad thing, but it needs to be coupled with action and your own choices.

If you don't take action and just let destiny unfold on its own, you end up losing control over your life. Instead of being the main character in your own story, you're a spectator. The challenges that come your way don't serve as chances to grow; they become obstacles that hold you back.

The destination isn't predetermined; it shifts and changes based on the path you choose to follow. Having faith that destiny will lead you somewhere good is a dominant driving force, but it must be paired with action and not passive acceptance. When you actively shape your path, believing that the future holds promise while taking steps to ensure it, this approach has the same transformative power as hope. In fact, faith in destiny and hope may be one and the same—both are driven by a vision of a better future, and both require your commitment to making that vision a reality.

The Need for Tech Reviewers

- October 02, 2024

MKBHD, also known as Marques Brownlee, has been dubbed several times as "the man who decides what tech everyone in America buys." That term is not an overstatement. Marques has a lot of power when you zoom in and look at the effect he has had on several companies. Take the Rabbit R1, for example. The Rabbit R1 was meant to be a product that changed the AI industry—a device eventually meant to replace smartphones. However, Marques' review was brutally honest, bashing its functionality, design flaws, and lack of practicality. The people took notice, and the negative feedback from his review sent waves through the startup, putting them on the brink of collapse. When MKBHD critiques a product, the entire industry listens, and his influence can make or break even the most visionary tech companies.

Ven phones made 3 years ago. His evaluation led to widespread backlash against the company, putting on full display the power reviewers hold over consumer trust. Maini's recent takedown of Geo-Cleanse, a product falsely claiming to protect against 5G radiation, demonstrated his ability to sniff out scams and protect his audience from falling prey to gimmicks, while entertaining them at the same time.

Similarly, Arun Maini, better known as Mrwhosetheboss, has a massive bubble of influence in the tech area. His meticulous and thorny reviews combined with a sense of humor that his audience has grown to love can sway public opinion in seconds. When he reviewed the Freedom Phone—a device marketed as a privacy-first alternative to mainstream smartphones—he exposed it for being a knockoff phone with specs below e

These tech reviewers serve a key role in today's technology dominated world. In an industry filled to its eyes with false information and hyperbole marketing claims, tech reviewers like MKBHD and Mrwhosetheboss serve as a reliable firewall for consumers. Their neck-breathing reviews are more than just what they feel—they are well-researched analyses that provide viewers with the stuff they need to know to make a decision that is in support of their best interests. Holding tech companies accountable through the individuals we trust is the only way to make sure that tech going forward is consumer-based. As someone who also critiques technology—but on a relatively smaller scale—I myself appreciate the value of honesty and transparency in this field. Even at the ground level, the burden of being balanced, well-informed, and useful to spectators is real. We're all working towards the same goal: filtering out the noise to enable others to make better decisions.

The Impact of LeBron James

- September 15, 2024

LeBron James. The face of the NBA, and has been for 20 years. Coming out of high school with the expectation of being the chosen one, no one ever expected The King to completely shatter those expectations, surpassing them faster than him chasing down his pray for a chase-down block. But don't take my word for it.

Let's talk numbers. His career field goal percentage of 50.6% is an insane statistic for someone who has taken 29,313 shots in his career. Sure, doing this is in a single season is pretty normal, but doing so for a career spanning 21 years while averaging over 27 points per game is epochal.

But LeBron is not just a scorer. His career averages, not season averages, career averages, of 7 rebounds and 7 assists per game make him one of the deadliest offensive players to ever touch the rim. Don't even get me started on LeBron's defensive side. His perimeter defense combined with paint prowess is sufficient to guard small points like Steph Curry and also dominant power forwards like Giannis Antetokounmpo. Then there's The Block.

"The Block."

"Iguodala to Curry, back to Iguodala, up for the layup… OOHHHHH blocked by James! LeBron James with the rejection!"

LeBron's iconic chase-down block on Andre Iguodala in Game 7 of the 2016 NBA Finals is not just a something the NBA Instagram page puts up for views; it is a defining moment in NBA history. The play amazingly showcases LeBron's blend of athleticism, timing, and sheer determination. At that moment, with the score tied, less than two minutes remaining, and it being an elimination game, he covered nearly 88 feet at full sprint and then leaped with his head higher than the rim to swat Iguodala's layup like a flu. This single play altered the trajectory of the game, the series, and even the legacies of everyone involved. Take that Max Kellerman.

LeBron James' missed 2-pointer against the Washington Wizards was like a jolt to all the subjects of King James. With just under six seconds left and the game tied, he had the perfect opportunity to end the game from mid-range—one of the easiest shots possible. But this time, the ball bounced off the rim, and for a moment, it felt like LeBron had choked, finally succumbed to the immense expectations that had been placed upon him from the minute he entered the league as an 18-year-old.

Yet, it was what happened next that really displays LeBron's amazing ability to have no nerves. To have ice cold blood in his veins.

With seconds left on the clock, he dribbled down the court, eased himself, and under the extreme pressure of the moment, drained a last minute 3-pointer over two defenders, securing the win.

This sequence, where he transitioned from the dude who missed an open mid-range to the greatest player basketball has ever seen in a heartbeat, re-molded the way I looked at him.

After dominating the NBA for two decades, you'd think he'd be beyond mistakes, but it's moments like these that remind us of his humanity.

LeBron's shot wasn't just about winning the game; it was a testament to the relentless pursuit of redemption, a narrative that has shadowed his entire career—from coming back to Cleveland to the comeback against the greatest NBA roster of all time.

This has taught me that no matter what the odds are, no matter how many times you fall, in the end, people will remember how you got back up.

Ethics of Time Travel

- August 13, 2024

Time travel. Sounds like the ultimate power. But time travel isn't just about revisiting the past—it's a Pandora's box of ethical dilemmas and moral paradoxes that shake up our fundamental ideas of what we consider to be right.

If we just take a peek at the idea, it seems like walking the road of time would let us prevent disasters, or meet people who are passed a long time ago. However, once you start tinkering with the timeline, things unravel faster than you can say "oops". What if shifting the location of a chair leads to nuclear war? What if saving one life means sacrificing another? The ripple effect of even the smallest change could reconfigure history in ways we can't possibly predict.

Take one of the more famous time travel stories out there: Flashpoint. The flash has had enough. He runs back in time, saves his mom from dying, and thinks, “finally, a happy ending for me!”

Nope.

There is now a war between the kingdoms of the sea and land, and the most famous superheroes of all time, Batman and Superman, are now dead.

Then there’s the question of responsibility. Why should the flash get to decide whom to save and who not to? Why shouldn’t he save someone else’s parent?

Also, why should we impose our ethical rules and morals on the people of that time period? This “changing the past” idea stems from the fact that humanity always considers itself to be superior than others. “This guy made this decision which was wrong, but the one I’ll make is right, so I should fix it.”

The past is not the only thing at stake. If we could glance behind the curtain in front of us, it would mean that the future is predetermined. Or would it mean that, due to the observer effect, the future that I witnessed is already erased from existence, along with the people of that timeline?

Time travel also raises questions about the nature of justice. If we could go back and undo a crime, would that erase the suffering it caused? Or would it merely shift the burden of that suffering onto someone else? And what about the potential for exploitation? The people with the power to manipulate time could use it to serve their own interests, enlarging the already gigantic gap between the rich and the poor.

#Drip20

What if One Person Could Take Away the World's nuclear weapons?

- August 05, 2024

Let's say you can just whip the nuclear weapons of the world out of the window. But before you decide, let's think about it. What moral concerns will race through your mind if you did do it?

The destruction capacity of these weapons cannot be matched, posing an eternal threat to not just humanity, but the earth itself. Removing this monstrosity might seem like the type of question which you can answer without your senses. However, consider the delicate balance of power maintained by nuclear weapons. Countries like the USA, Russia, and North Korea, armed with vast arsenals, deter large-scale wars through mutually assured destruction. Yoinking these weapons could destabilize global peace, as nations might turn to conventional or even more insidious warfare, believing they can strike without nuclear retaliation.

Can One Sole Person Decide This?

The enormity of this decision begs the question: can one sole person wield such power responsibly? Deciding to eliminate all nuclear weapons isn't just a technical or political choice; it's a moral and ethical dilemma. One person, no matter how wise or well-informed, takes their own biases and selfish needs with them. The decision to disarm must consider global perspectives and future implications. Relying on a single individual to make this decision risks oversimplifying this extremely nuanced issue.

If one person does decide it, what separates them from a dictator, a tyrant? Isn’t this the exact reason why democracy was created in the first place?

And let’s say we look at it from the other side. This person took a survey of the entire world population. 70% of them said yes to disarmament. But does the general population always know what’s best for them? In 1920, the United States government introduced the 18th Amendment to The Constitution, banning the manufacture, sale, and transportation of alcoholic beverages. At the time, the general public was really pushing for it, thinking it would reduce crime, abuse, and fix the general order of the country. 13 years later, organized crime, smuggling of goods, and a general disregard for the law was monumentally high, forcing the public and the government to backtrack their words.

How is this any different? Maybe the public does want the threat of nuclear weapons gone, but have no clue what kind of power vacuum it will leave.

#Drip121

The Importance of Memes

- July 28, 2024

While scrolling through your internet feed in front of your friends, you suddenly start laughing. The first thing your friends will say is: “Show me the meme.”.

Memes have become an elemental part of our daily digital interactions. Not even digital, actually. People have started quoting memes in real life. “I swear on skibidi” or “Bruh”.

They are not just random pictures with funny captions but a hilarious yet relatable form of communication that reflects our society's collective cognizance. Memes put, not just funny cats, but also heavily nuanced, global problems into a white text box and an image of Dwayne Johnson raising an eyebrow.

Memes are the modern equivalent of the ancient hieroglyphs, but way funnier. These digital artifacts allow us to spread a message by breaking traditional ideas. They are concise, relatable, and often hilarious. Yet, beneath the humor lies a powerful tool for social commentary. Think about the last time a meme made you laugh. Was it just the joke, or was there an underlying truth that resonated with you? That’s the magic of memes—they blend humor with insight.

However, memes can also amplify stereotypes and misinformation. When a meme goes viral, it can spread ideas faster than you can say "that's offensive". This perpetuation can reinforce societal norms or challenge them, depending on the message. Take an echo chamber in support of Batman, for example. It is difficult to comprehend how fast an offensive meme about Superman can reach from one corner of the Internet to another.

The oversimplification that makes the very foundation of memes can also lead to misinterpretation. One that is funny to a person might be offensive to another, highlighting the cultural and contextual subtleties that shape our perception.

Consider the impact of memes during major events like elections or social movements. Memes can serve as rallying cries, uniting people with a shared message. Like for the past few weeks, so many memes about Project 2025 have been shared in so many group chats. Now people actually know what it is, and they can vote with this information in mind, spreading this info to other people at the same time.

They can encapsulate complex political ideologies in a single image or phrase, making them accessible to a broader audience. This democratization of content creation and distribution empowers individuals to participate in cultural and political discourse in ways that were previously not even dreamt of.

However, this democratization comes with a dark side. Memes can be weaponized to spread disinformation and manipulate public opinion. The same tools that enable us to share a laugh can also be used to sow seeds of discord. Take the same Superman meme. Imagine if it was shared in a Superman subreddit. Or the actual DC Comics subreddit. The chaos that would ensue from it would be like a tsunami that mods would have a field day keeping at bay.

The Unbalanced Sock Conundrum

- July 12, 2024

Feeling lost in a sea of unmatched socks? You're not alone! A recent study (conducted by yours truly, at 3 am with a flashlight) reveals a staggering 87% of teenagers experience this existential sock crisis. Scientists (aka my neighbor who folds laundry) are baffled. Are these lonely socks whispers from a parallel dimension? Do they yearn for freedom, or perhaps a tiny sock revolution? The world may never know. So next time you face this socky conundrum, just remember: you're not crazy, you're a participant in the great sock mystery. Stay strong, friends.

Cancel Cancel Culture

- July 09, 2024

A place where a single mistake can lead to the destruction of both your professional and social standing. It seems bad, right? Well, this is what cancel culture is. Platforms like Twitter and Instagram have become stadiums where any controversial opinion you come up with can lead to utter and complete annihilation. While intended to promote accountability, cancel culture often leaves no room for context, growth, or redemption. It is shockingly similar to a lifelong exile from medieval times.

This might sound like an efficient way to ensure people are held responsible for their actions, and sometimes it really does work. However, it lacks nuance. When someone is "canceled," more often than not, they are condemned, banished from life as we know it. It may result in them losing their job, friends, and opportunities over a single incident, tweet, or just liking the wrong post.

Think about the content you share, the tweets you like, the comments you leave. They all play a role in perpetuating cancel culture. It's not just about highlighting wrongdoings; it creates an atmosphere where fear of mistakes stagnates genuine expression and open dialogue, the whole point of these platforms in the first place. Being part of this "Online Justice League" skews our moral sense, making it difficult to distinguish between rightful accountability and being part of a hive mind.

So, the next time you consider joining a digital riot, or try to bash on a person just because everyone else is, remember that you're not just part of a social movement. You're influencing the values of the online community, potentially leading to positive change or unwarranted destruction. Strive for understanding and context. Reject the idea that one mistake defines a person. This approach fosters a true culture. It's one of true accountability and growth, rather than one where everybody has the same thought, and the ones with less popular ones are silenced.

We Need to be Bored

- July 04, 2024

When was the last time you sat down, and did nothing? Absolutely nothing. Can't remember? Yeah, me neither. You may be wondering, whoever needs to be bored? But sit down and think about it, for a second.

Isaac Newton. He conceived the idea of gravity while sitting under a tree. J.K. Rowling. She created the concept of a book set in a magic school, while waiting for her train.

History is filled with examples of boredom leading to great decisions. When you do nothing, and distractions aren't keeping your mind occupied, the brain starts to wander. It is able to go to places where it never could before, because it was always caught up in one thing or the other. Isaac Newton didn't have a burst of dopamine just sitting in his pocket. That's why he was able to make one of the most groundbreaking discoveries in the history of science.

Walk back into the time-stream, to when you had a brilliant idea or a sudden solution to a problem. More often than not, these moments came when you were not actively trying to think of them—maybe while showering, walking, or just daydreaming. When the brain is allowed to relax and drift, it accesses the huge creative pool that has been waiting for you.

But in today's world, we rarely allow ourselves this luxury. Either you have to go to a party, or finish that essay you haven't touched in a week.

But this is the use of humans. Being creative. Any AI can finish an essay while following the exact guidelines to get an A on it. You, on the other hand, can push those guidelines. Bend them. Break them.

Even back in the caveman era, humans survived because they created spears, axes, used fire in such creative ways that changed civilization.

So, the next time you find yourself reaching for that phone just to move your thumb in two directions, don't. Rather, just sit, and let your brain explore the vast, endless tub of creative juices, which have been calling you for your entire life.

What Should We Watch?

- June 30, 2024

Remember the days when your biggest TV dilemma was choosing between a few channels? Now, we're living in the golden age of streaming, with endless content at our fingertips. Netflix, Hulu, Disney+, HBO Max—the list goes on. But here's the catch: having too many choices can be just as paralyzing as having too few.

It's called the paradox of choice. With so many options available, deciding what to watch can become an overwhelming task. You spend more time scrolling through the catalog than actually enjoying a show or movie. The abundance of choice can lead to decision fatigue, where the act of choosing itself becomes exhausting.

Moreover, the pressure to pick the "right" show is real. With friends and social media constantly buzzing about the latest must-watch series, there's a fear of missing out (FOMO). This can turn what should be a relaxing activity into a stressful one. Instead of unwinding, you're anxious about staying up-to-date.

And let's not forget the cost. Subscribing to multiple streaming services can quickly add up, becoming more expensive than the old cable bundles we left behind. The promise of cutting the cord for cheaper entertainment is becoming a myth as more and more services enter the market, each with its exclusive content.

#Drip26

Social Media Echo Chambers

\- June 29, 2024

Imagine a world where every opinion you encounter aligns perfectly with your own. Sounds great, right? Wrong. Welcome to the world of social media echo chambers. Platforms like Twitter and Facebook, with their intricate algorithms, are designed to show you content that you are most likely to engage with, reinforcing your existing beliefs and preferences. It's like living in a bubble where everyone agrees with you.

But here's the catch: this bubble isn't harmless. It breeds polarization. When you only see content that aligns with your views, you become increasingly convinced that your perspective is the only correct one. Disagreements become not just debates but full-blown battles. Civil discourse? Out the window. The result? A society divided, with each faction entrenched in its own reality.

Take a step back and think about it. The stories you share, the posts you like, the comments you leave—they all contribute to the echo chamber. It's not just about seeing what you like; it's about never seeing what you don't like. This digital curation distorts our perception of reality, making it harder to understand and empathize with opposing viewpoints.

So, next time you scroll through your feed, remember: you're not just consuming content. You're shaping your worldview, for better or worse. Break out of the bubble. Seek diverse perspectives. Challenge your own beliefs. It's the only way to foster genuine understanding in an increasingly fragmented digital landscape.

#Drip27

Mr. Clutch, The Logo, and Mr. Outside

\- June 19, 2024

I have been a crazy fan of the NBA for nearly 4 years now. Funnily enough, the league itself did not grab my attention, but in fact, it was NBA 2k20, which my brother bought because it was on sale. He was familiar with the NBA, but I had no clue it even existed. After downloading this gigantic game, we grabbed our controllers and played our first game ever (after the tutorial, of course). He chose All-Time Warriors, and I chose All-Time Lakers. After just 2 quarters, I was in love with, not the game, but the players. Kobe's' mid-range. Magic's playmaking. Shaq's unbelievable dominance.

But the player I made 33 points and 11 assists with was Jerry West. His incredible shooting, playmaking, and inside game just made him work. Combine that with making the defenders dance like they were in a club and being able to guard someone twice his size, and you have The Logo.

Mr. Clutch was known to be extremely, extremely competitive. He is the only player in NBA history to be named the Finals MVP while being on the losing team. This feat requires the highest level of dedication and drive possible, combined with amazing skill and 0 luck.

As an executive for the Lakers, I have him to thank for one of the greatest duos of the NBA: Shaq and Kobe. He was also working as a consultant for the Warriors during their run which obliterated the league, further adding to his 11-foot resume.

#Drip28

Nuclear Power on Trial

\- June 16, 2024

Judge: Order in the court! Let the trial begin. This is The People v. Nuclear Power.

Prosecution: Your honor, I only have one word to start off my argument: Chernobyl.

Nuclear: Why is it that anytime anyone debates over this, Chernobyl is the first name to come up? It was one simple mistake.

Prosecution: Simple? Nearly 50 people died just because of the initial explosion. Dozens of others died later due to radiation-induced cancer. How is that simple? And one mistake? What about the Fukushima accident?

Nuclear: You say all of these things, but keep in mind, nuclear threat was the only reason WWII ended. I have helped save countless, countless, lives.

Prosecution: And how many had to die to achieve that? How many people have suffered due to the bombings of Hiroshima and Nagasaki?

Nuclear: A small price to pay for several years of peace.

Prosecution: You sound like every supervillain ever.

Nuclear: Objection. Not relevant.

Judge: Sustained.

Nuclear: And what about the energy that the smallest quantity of hydrogen can generate? This is actual, efficient, renewable energy. Say goodbye to coal.

Prosecution: Oh yeah? And what about all the radioactive waste? Is that good for the environment?

Nuclear: Put it hundreds of feet below the ground. It won't harm anyone, and it will naturally decay over time.

Prosecution: And where will the money to dig these holes, to get the people and equipment required to operate the nuclear plants, come from?

Nuclear: At first through investors, but eventually, through the energy we sell. Just like every other energy source.

Prosecution: What about the safety of the workers who have to dig holes this deep to dispose of the waste?

Nuclear: It's literally the same as when workers dig to get petroleum; your honor, the prosecution is just saying stuff for the sake of saying them.

Judge: Yeah alright, the defendant is not guilty. Prosecution, come up with better arguments next time.

#Drip29

My Brother Bought a Tesla

- June 14, 2024

I'll just say it: I'm not the kind of guy who would look at a Lamborghini and go, "which model is that?" No, I'm the kind of guy who would just be happy that he saw a Lamborghini.

So, you would think that when my brother told me that he bought a Tesla I would be like, "huh, that's cool, I guess."

But a Tesla for me is way better than a Lamborghini. "Why dost thou make such an outrageous claim?"

Before you take out your swords, let me explain. I do not like driving cars. The minute I put my hands on the steering wheel, my body goes into petrified mode. Even if the road is empty, I'm scared I'll crash the car into the curb.

Tesla's full self-driving though, that changes things. I no longer need to worry about steering, switching lanes, or just driving in general. The car does that for me. So, ironically enough, my dream car turns out to be a car… which I don't drive.

#Drip30

Minecraft: The Greatest Video Game Ever Made

- June 14, 2024

Minecraft, the most sold video game of all time. It beat GTA V, Tetris, and Wii Sports to be the most famous video game of all time.

When I first saw someone play it, I was like, "Seriously? These are blocks. Literally blocks. You break blocks, you place blocks, you click on zombies with a sword. How in the world is this such a popular game?"

But then, something changed. I decided to give it a try, if only to understand the hype. It was one of those moments where you go in with negative expectations, just waiting to stop doing it. And boy, was I in for a surprise. As soon as I started playing, I realized that Minecraft is not just about blocks. It's about creativity, freedom, and intelligence.

As I delved deeper, I discovered that Minecraft is like a digital playground where your imagination is the only limit. Want to build a replica of the Eiffel Tower? Go ahead. How about playing Quidditch using mods? Absolutely possible. Feeling adventurous? Dive into survival mode and face the challenges of the wild, from gathering resources, to not dying of hunger, to battling creepers and endermen. The game offers so many different ways to play, and each experience can be completely unique.

Then there's the community aspect. Minecraft has a massive and dedicated fanbase. Players share their creations, mods, and custom maps, adding even more variety to the game. Whether you're exploring a mod that completely changes the game, or joining a multiplayer server which is literally multiplayer Pokemon in Minecraft, there's always something new to experience. People have even worked together to create entire cities, theme parks, and even functioning computers within the game. FUNCTIONAL COMPUTERS! With just the stuff in the game. From scratch. That is insane!

Privacy

- June 09, 2024

In a time where 85% of your life runs through Instagram, no stalker is ever going to peek through your windows. The stories you post, showing off that you're in Malibu sipping on Mojitos? These never would've happened without the technological age. Think about it. Posting these stories is the same as telling everyone you know, (don't even get me started on public accounts) "hey! I'm currently in paradise, right at this spot. Let's split some nachos."

And this is the stuff you send out willingly. When you log into the Starbucks Wi-Fi and buy a $100 body pillow using your credit card? A guy sitting in the corner with a hood on his head sipping on a Frappuccino could be going ham at a

Gucci store next door. It's as easy sniffing out the bits you sent through the router and just letting them diffuse into the hacker's laptop.

It's not even individuals doing this stuff. Remember Mark Zuckerberg? The human robot? Yeah, his social media platform Facebook has gotten into at least 8000 controversies regarding stealing the data of the user's. And when you save your credit card information in Chrome? One data leak and your bank account get drained to 0.

#Drip32

Apple and AI

- - June 09, 2024

Being the Apple fanboy that I am, Apple has definitely fallen behind in the AI race when comparing with Microsoft, Samsung, and Google. Google and Microsoft surging ahead is something I can live with. But not Samsung. Hey, I have nothing against Samsung, but my loyalties lie with Apple.

Having said that, I do feel that Apple should stay away from any gimmicky stuff and concentrate on stuff that is truly going to help the billions of users that use its devices, including me.

We have the WWDC starting in 2 days and I, for one, can't wait for the keynote. I make it a point to watch all the keynotes live and this one will be no different. Plus, this time, the developer conference is all online, so looking to attend as many sessions as possible will be one of my priorities.

#Drip33

Perspective Matters

\- - May 23, 2024

Apple. One of the most valuable companies on earth. To their fanbase, they can do no wrong. Whether that is restricting user's to just the App Store for their app needs, or taking a gigantic 30% cut from the app developers, Apple themselves, along with their fans, have always stood by their decisions. Until now.

The infamous Crush ad. The intended sentiment being that all of the people's hard work has gone into making the iPad. Yeah sure. Makes sense. View it from another perspective, however, and it transforms itself into something completely different: crushing the sculptures and the keyboard, as they are old news. Now, after crushing its competition, the iPad stands alone. The iPad can do everything those things can do.

This little slip up made Apple apologize. Because they did not consider what the ad would seem like to someone who actually does play the instruments, or who makes sculptures.

There are several other examples that remain, of course, but this gives a good gist of the problem. Not consulting many people will always lead to this problem. If you don't have a large sample size while testing the product, you won't know what your creation will look like to the rest of the world.

India's Standardized Testing

- May 16, 2024

JEE. NEET. The most famous examples of standardized tests. These tests are shaping not only India, but the world these days, being an integral part, and in many cases the only part, in deciding the future of a student. While they are very convenient, the added pressure is one of the biggest factors for student suicides in India.

It just takes one test, one piece of paper, to decide whether a student can go to college or not. That's too much stuff to be decided by something so insignificant. One test. All it takes for one kid's dream to go poof. I cannot stress this enough. The 2 years of 11-hour-study-session-filled days all boil down to one day. And what if that day your pen runs out of ink? You get in a car accident? You either wait three or, if you were going to give it in April, NINE whole months. Plenty of time for the barometer in your head to rise up to 100.

These tests are one of the most rigorous ones as well. They are known as one of the hardest ever, and genuinely test a student's knowledge. Knowing so much about either chemistry, physics, and math or biology is no easy task, especially not for anyone not suited and tuned for an environment harboring the greatest minds of the generation.

These tests are also a great indicator of a future pioneer's drive and want to achieve. If you are willing to sit for 11 hours a day for 2 years straight just studying for a single test, you are sure to reach places.

Virtual Reality on Trial

- May 08, 2024

Judge: Order in the court! Who is the defendant today?

VR: Virtual reality, your honor. Also known as the future of humanity.

Prosecutor: Future, my foot. I think we all have seen what Mark looks like in virtual reality, and let's just say most people prefer slender-man to virtual Zuck.

VR: So, the technology is still being perfected, sue me. People were skeptical about removing the home button, weren't they?

Prosecutor: That is hardly the same thing! There is a huge difference between removing a button and shifting the medium through which humanity interacts!

VR: Your honor, tell me, wouldn't it be wonderful if you didn't have to come down to court for every little case that ends up on your desk? You could just stay in bed but still interact with everyone that should be present in the court.

People won't have to leave their important matters just for jury duty.

Judge: You're not wrong. Wearing this huge black robe at this temperature is no joke. I could get on board with judging without budging.

Prosecutor: But your honor, what about seeing the defendant with your own 2 eyes? You won't be able make out the facial expressions, seeing the person in the eye and knowing whether they are guilty or not. Nothing can replicate the real-life eyesight.

VR: Oh, come on. The inability to make out emotions is exactly what is required these days! People can fake emotions. It is important to be objective, to look at just the evidence and decide.

Judge: True.

Prosecutor: What about identity? People can modify themselves to look like anything. Anything. Do you even realize how much danger that poses to society as we know it?

VR: What do you even mean by "society as we know it"? Society changes with each era, and arguably for the better. And this is for the better. People can look like anything they want. They would be able to interact without their physical limitations. If they feel that they resemble a Stormtrooper better than their current body, then so be it! Who are you to decide what people should look like? Plastic surgery exists, doesn't it? And what about people with disabilities? They will finally be able to do everything on an equal level to everyone else!

Judge: All right, all right, that will be enough. I have seen how Virtual Reality can harm and benefit us and I have concluded that it obviously does not pose a threat to us. In its current state, it serves no more purpose than Roblox. And if it does take shape of what the defendant says it will, I see the advantages greatly outweighing the drawbacks. Court adjourned.

#Drip36

I'm Hulk's Anger Management Tutor

\- May 02, 2024

Before you say anything, I already asked Bruce. I'm free to advertise myself as Hulk's "associate".

So, here are my anger management tips that keep even the world's angriest man (literally) in check:

Feel like smashing some things? Imagine that those things are actually those that are really valuable to those. For example, if you want to smash a table, just imagine your MacBook on that table. You surely don't want to smash that, do you?

Thor left his hammer on the toilet seat again? First of all, find a different bathroom. Then, take a deep breath. Deep breath. I know that you will be very, very tempted to defecate on Thor's stuff. Stop. Think how Thor will react when he finds out you pooped on his limited edition Noose the Moose. Raining down lightning from the heavens? Calling Heimdall through the Bifrost? Definitely. You know how boring that guy is. “I just saw a poor plant give its life just so you people could put leaves on pizza”. Oh, shut up.

For now, these are all the beans I can spill. I will eventually post more, but this is all for now. Anyways, I wouldn’t want Abomination to see these tips, would I?

Abomination, if you need some tips, gimme a call. I know the friction between you and hulk, but I won't tell if you won't.

#Drip37

I'm Spider-Man's Laundry Guy

- April 25, 2024

So, you know how the Green Goblin has a glider guy, or how Cap has a shield cleaner guy?

Well, I'm Spider-Man's laundry guy. I'm one of the few people that he trusts with his secret identity, and of course I'm honored and all but… did it really have to be me? There are so many laundromats in New York, and still, Pe- sorry, Spider-Man (whoops), just had to pick me. Some days it's slime that a hater threw on his suit (and they had to use green slime, you know, the one that contrasts the most with the costume). Some days it's condensed Goblin Laughing Gas. I was laughing so much that an old lady outside Marriott took it personally and called security on me.

How is condensing a laughing gas even scientifically possible? Leave it to the Goblin to find ways to do this, but not solve world hunger. Supervillains these days, I tell you.

Okay okay, I know what you're going to say: "He's Spider-Man. He saves your butt every other day. The least you could do is wash his damn clothes."

I get it. But I need to make an honest living. I have lost around 200 bucks just because the Webhead's attire takes 16 hours to wash. and 16 more to dry. I have got a black hole (i.e., my stomach) to feed.

Yes, I have tried asking Spidey to endorse my laundry business, but he has always said that it will attract danger, people like Doc Ock. Frankly, I'll take it. Ock's suit really needs a cleaning. He literally looks homeless.

#Drip38

Writer's Block

- April 11, 2024

Everybody goes through this. Whether it be writing a book, a Drip (whoops), or just trying to send a text: writer's block is a major hinderance consuming the people of Earth (and probably Mars). It's what's stopping from sending out a beautifully written (hopefully) Drip out right now.

And it doesn't just have to be in the matters of writing. People get "stuck" all the time, everywhere. Someone could have a fractured foot stopping them from practicing track and field events. A person may not know what they want to do as a career, impeding their supply of money.

It's different names, but the same thing in essence.

#Drip39

Social Media Algorithms

\- March 08, 2024

Judge: Order, order, order! Who is the defendant today?

Prosecution: Social media algorithms, your honor. The code culpable for narcotizing the entire population of the planet, making them no less than the zombies that plants are a little too used to beating. The defendant is representing all social media platforms, including Facebook, YouTube, Instagram, and the likes.

Judge: Instagram? I'm not watching Instagram! Who said that?

Defendant: The prosecution your honor.

Prosecution: No, I didn't! Shut up! Ahem. Forgive me, your honor. Shall we get started?

Judge: Go ahead with the prosecution.

Prosecution: Your honor, as you and I both know, we can't put down Instagram Reels, or TikTok. I got so used to swiping up, I once flung my toothpaste off my brush! The average person spends 2 hours and 24 minutes on social media, either envying their friends' trip to Maldives, or watching a dog dance to 'Dance till You're Dead'.

Defendant: Your honor, is it really my fault if people choose to spend their time on these apps? Let me ask you a question: If a man shoots someone using a pistol, do you arraign the man, or the pistol?

Prosecution: If the pistol was capable of releasing dopamine in the man's brain, then yeah, I would blame the gun.

Defendant: Objection! That's irrelevant! If some humans lack the willpower to overcome something as trivial as dopamine-

Prosecution: Willpower my butt! You ha-

Judge: Order in the court! Prosecution, continue with your argument.

Prosecution: A thousand pardons, your honor. I now call The Myanmar Crisis 2017 to the stand.

Ms. Crisis, was there hostility towards the Rohingya Muslim minority in your country in 2017?

Myanmar Crisis 2017: Yes, there was.

Prosecution: Did this culminate into hate speech and, eventually, violence?

Myanmar Crisis 2017: Yes, it did.

Prosecution: Were there reports that Facebook "played a determining role" in the hate speech and eventual violence?

Myanmar Crisis 2017: Yes, there were.

Prosecution: I rest my case.

Judge: Defendant, you're looking guilty. Wanna question the witness?

Defendant: Yes, your honor, I do 'wanna' question the witness.

Ms. Crisis, tell me, in what time period did these ethnic divides exist?

Myanmar Crisis 2017: The 19th century were the first records, but it's highly likely they existed before then.

Defendant: Did Facebook exist at that time?

Myanmar Crisis 2017: No, it did not.

Defendant: I rest my case.

Prosecution: So, what? Gasoline can stay as it is for a long time, but a spark is what causes the fire!

Defendant: The spark is not Facebook. The spark is the people on Facebook. People are the problem, every single time.

Prosecution: Your algorithm brings hate speech to the front page! The terrorists are there, but you're the one who is transporting the terrorists right in front of the people's faces!

Defendant: People want me to bring this stuff to their faces! They know what they are signing up for when they accept the user agreement and privacy policy. I only show the truth, and people want the truth. It's not my problem that the truth can affect people the wrong way sometimes.

Prosecution: Oh, the truth? So, what about the deep fakes you help "bring to people's faces" of The President robbing a Kentucky Diner?

Judge: That's it, we're straying off-topic. I have reached the verdict. I find the defendant… NOT GUILTY! Mainly because I have to catch a livestream right now, but whatever.

Fear vs Inspiration to Stop Crime

- December 12, 2023

What's the first thing you imagine when you think of Batman? A tall, dark, imposing figure, perhaps? That's what is meant to appear in your head, at least. It's the main idea behind Batman. Fear. It's how he fights crime; how he will eventually end it. And it definitely has its upsides.

Using intimidation as a way for justice may be frowned upon, but it gets the job done. Intimidation as a technique is so effective (for Batman), that supervillains stopped committing their crime just from a look from Batman. Just a look. You can't tell me that that isn't crazy efficient. And let's face it, if Batman breaks 5 of your bones while you were attempting a bank robbery, you wouldn't want to do that again, would you?

Now forget fear and picture this: Batman, not just a caped crusader but a beacon of inspiration. A symbol that transcends fear and instills hope in the hearts of Gotham's citizens. It's not about a menacing look; it's about being a source of positive change.

In a city shrouded by the darkness of crime, Batman, as an inspiring figure, becomes the catalyst for a collective movement. He empowers the community to rise against the shadows and actively participate in shaping a safer Gotham. It's not just about waiting for a hero; it's about realizing that the power to bring change lies within every citizen inspired by Batman's commitment to justice.

Furthermore, the impact of inspiration extends far beyond immediate results. Batman's actions become a rallying cry, cultivating a legacy of goodness that resonates through the generations. It's not merely about stopping criminal activities; it's about instilling values that endure, creating a cultural shift towards compassion, resilience, and the unwavering belief that even in the darkest times, individuals can make a difference.

Fear will only lead to a short-term change. However, being a source of inspiration can, and has, compelled other people to take up the mantle of the Batman after Bruce Wayne's retirement or passing. That, will truly go a long way towards the goal of ending all crime. Batman will be a hero, for both the people he has inspired, and those supervillains he has spared and genuinely helped, not just beaten to a pulp.

While all of the above is true, a quote from Alfred (Michael Cane), Batman's butler, will sum up what I'm trying to convince you of-

"Endure, Master Wayne. Take it. They'll hate you for it, but that's the point of Batman, he can be the outcast. He can make the choice that no one else can make: the right choice."

#Drip41

Should Superheroes be Under Government Supervision?

- December 04, 2023

Okay, imagine you're in a world of superheroes, swinging between buildings and trying to do what's right. Now, there's this talk about whether these heroes should be working for the government. Here's my take on it, considering what some heroes might say.

Look, heroes have their own moral compass, and tying them to government agendas might mess that up. If they're on the government payroll, they could end up doing things that serve politics instead of what's genuinely right. We want heroes making decisions based on what's best for everyone, not just what some suits want.

Plus, heroes often find themselves in messy situations where they gotta bend the rules to save the day. If they're tied to government paperwork, it could slow them down. Sometimes you gotta act fast, and bureaucracy doesn't do fast very well.

Imagine, Thanos is invading the world, and the Hulk first has to attend a council meeting to decide whether the Avengers should fight Thanos or not. Even if you do put a VETO power in place for situations like this, to what extent can the person holding the VETO power use this? Who decides who gets the VETO power? Will it be a singular person or a country? The person holding the VETO power will be the most powerful (wo)man on Earth, who will be able to control the world's superheroes; will the general public really trust a government official to have this kind of power?

And let's talk about power. We've seen how it can corrupt. If heroes are under government control, there's a risk they could lose their independence and become just another piece in the bureaucratic puzzle. We need them to stay true to their cause, not become government yes-men.

In the end, it's like this massive jigsaw puzzle where each piece represents a choice heroes make. Should they punch the clock for the government or keep flying solo? Considering the moral maze, they navigate; it seems like tying heroes to the government might not be the best move.

Does God Exist?

- October 27, 2023

First of all, I personally don't believe in God. Either capital G god or small g gods (like Ram, Zeus, Jesus, etc.). I am an atheist. However, that doesn't mean I resent people who do believe in God, or think 'that guy's a moron.' No. You want to believe in God, go ahead. You want to enforce your ideas upon those who don't want to believe? Sorry, that's where I draw my line.

This argument is a multifaceted debate, being iterated over countless times in sundry texts throughout the years. The interpretation of "God" has varied across the time periods, notable ones being the Roman Gods, the Greek Gods, Jesus, the Hindu Gods, Egyptian Gods, and numerous more.

One side of this debate catechizes whether this is merely a misrepresentation of gods, and that these all are one and the same. That there is One Supreme Being, and humans, who subconsciously tend to put divides between themselves, 'see' different gods.

Another side of this diversified coin indicates that all gods different, and occupy the same, “divine power”, all of them balancing the cosmic see-saw. This rationale contrasts with the idea of a monarch and their followers. The more apostles you have, the more powerful you are.

Some disciples argue that humans, the animals, and the Earth have been hand crafted to perfection. They seem to have specific designs to meet their needs, and nature seems to be too random for this prodigious design, that is humans. There has to be a higher being that has made everything, from bacteria to elephants to everything in between.

And then there is my point of view. My belief. There probably are higher life forms. Life forms that far exceed the technological and mental capabilities of humans. But they did not create us. Nothing in nature is random. Everything can be predicted. Even something that seems random, like a coin toss, can be predicted if you pay close attention to the force applied, the force the wind puts on the coin, the amount of turns it takes, everything. So, is it really that unbelievable that nature came together perfectly to make us? There might be a few trillion failed attempts at making a possible Earth. Ours is the one in which all the variables fit. In which all the debris collected in the perfect amount. In which fatal asteroids were conveniently diverted from the Earth thanks to Jupiter.

However, a lot of people believe in God. A lot of people turn to God in times of hardship, when they have no one else to turn to. Even if God is make believe, what's so bad about it? A little faith never harmed anyone.

Batman's No Kill-Rule

- October 20, 2023

In the main DC Universe, Batman's no-kill policy is an unyielding principle, a vital part of his character that raises thought-provoking questions. Despite the moral complexities it introduces, his willingness to stick to this code is deeply rooted in his ideals and experiences.

Batman's commitment to the no-kill policy reflects his unwavering belief in the justice system. He firmly believes that the determination of guilt and the delivery of punishment should be a responsibility borne by society, not by an individual. He resists the urge to become both the judge and the executioner, believing justice should be upheld through lawful processes rather than personal vengeance. This stance positions Batman as a vigilante and a symbol of hope, emphasizing that the law must prevail over lawlessness.

Turning our attention to the "Batman Who Laughs" universe, we encounter a stark example of what transpires when Batman deviates from his no-kill policy. In this parallel reality, Batman succumbs to temptation, killing the Joker. The outcome is nothing short of catastrophic. Joker releases a toxin upon his death that converts Batman into the Joker.

It's as if all of Batman's immense strength and intelligence are merged with the Joker's uncontrolled evil, creating the "Batman Who Laughs." This horrifying character becomes the embodiment of chaos, essentially a dark reflection of Batman himself. The consequences are disastrous in a world where the Joker's malevolence is allowed to run rampant, unconstrained by Batman's moral code. The entire universe spirals into unrelenting darkness and bedlam.

In an alternate reality known as the "Grim Knight" universe, Batman, shaped by a defining moment where he took the life of his parents' killer, Joe Chill, embarks on a much darker path than his Prime Earth counterpart. Bearing the burden of his lethal choice, this Batman becomes a relentless and merciless vigilante. He forgoes his traditional no-kill policy and adopts extreme tactics, wiping out prominent crime bosses and leaving a trail of chaos in his wake. The Grim Knight embodies a ruthless brand of justice, igniting fear in the criminal underworld while drawing the condemnation of those who question the ethics of his actions, including GCPD Lieutenant Jim Gordon. In this grim and unrelenting universe, Batman's unyielding commitment to his moral code has been replaced by a far more brutal form of crime-fighting, setting the stage for a dramatic showdown with Commissioner Gordon, who stands as a beacon of unwavering principles in a city teetering on the precipice of darkness.

Anxious to Come, Mortified to Go

- September 17, 2023

This is the story of my Round Square Exchange Program, to The Brookhouse School, Nairobi, Kenya.

In the depths of my being, the journey commenced from the very moment I reluctantly stepped into the car, the vehicle that would carry me towards the threshold of emotions and uncertainty—the airport. Each step closer propelled me into a realm where individuals depart, a domain where uncertainty looms large, and the return is not always promised—the airport.

Ascending the stairwell to the awaiting flight, my thoughts were consumed by a whirlwind of conflicting emotions. Was this ascent leading me toward the annihilation of my familiar social landscape, or was it a climb toward my personal salvation? The domestic flight passed with deceptive ease, but the realization of departing my homeland sent tremors through my legs, causing even my ordinary sports shoes to quiver.

Seventeen long hours and fifteen anxious minutes later, I touched down in Nairobi, and the moment of truth beckoned—the dreaded immigration. Anxiety gnawed at me. Would they accuse me of being an unaccompanied minor, an offense in Kenya? Would they declare my visa null and order my deportation to the US, a nation distant from my current Indian abode? A storm of worrisome possibilities thundered through my mind, including the absurd notion that my phone could be mistaken for a concealed explosive. Yet, to my disbelief, the immigration officers scarcely asked me a question, waving me through after a cursory glance at my visa and passport. Joy surged within me, an exultant tide that carried me past the gates, a triumphant smile etched on my face, ready to face the enigmas this foreign land held.

Upon reaching the school, conversations with the administrative staff transpired, guiding me to the room that would cradle my existence for the next one and a half months. Inside, I encountered two fellow souls—Ben and Juan Diego Mora. Ben, a student of the school, and Juan, an exchange student hailing from Anglo-Colombiano, Colombia.

The initial week at the school unfurled, revealing a tapestry of individuals, each weaving their unique narratives into the fabric of my experience. Juan, Ben, and several other students imprinted their stories upon my consciousness.

As Friday's embrace drew near, I found myself in the company of my host, Adam Brown, venturing into the warmth of his family's embrace. Their hospitality, manifested in a splendidly prepared dinner upon my arrival, enveloped me in a comforting embrace.

School days melded into a tapestry of routine until the day of our first collective expedition emerged. Our destination: the breathtaking Masai Mara, a realm of awe-inspiring beauty where we beheld Africa's famed "Big Five" in their natural habitat. Despite my indifference toward wildlife, the enchantment of that experience transcended the boundaries of my expectations, etching a memory that sparkled with magic. Amidst the adventure, camaraderie blossomed with classmates like Eyed and Paul, the shared joy of music inadvertently leading to a playful reprimand when our boisterous melodies were discovered during the bus journey—a reprimand worth every note.

As the end of my exchange journey drew near, another escapade beckoned, this time to the ethereal Rift Valley. Accompanied by a class junior to ours, we forged unforgettable memories. Engaging with teachers and fellow students deepened our connections. Amidst this expedition, a hike to the pinnacle of a canyon cliff emerged as the crowning jewel, offering a vista of breathtaking beauty.

Yet, even in the throes of these adventures, a bitter reality loomed—the day of departure, an event laden with both anticipation and dread. The sadness of parting weighed heavily on my heart, for I knew that leaving meant bidding adieu to cherished souls.

In the tapestry of this journey, I unearthed a profound realization. Contrary to popular belief, the true challenge of an exchange does not solely lie in the solitary travel or the acclimatization to unfamiliar circumstances. No, the ultimate trial is bidding farewell to the individuals whose lives intertwined with mine, understanding that the odds of our paths crossing again may be slim.

An exchange, I now understand, mirrors the survival challenges of Minecraft. Embarking with naught but a clean slate—zero friends, zero familiarity with the terrain, and zero understanding of local customs—we embark on a quest. We must treasure each friendship forged, for they become the lifeblood of this journey. Every day unveils newfound appreciation for the mundane, the chores we'd seldom notice in our usual habitat, like laundering our clothes or navigating the intricacies of a plant-based diet. This voyage teaches us that despite the seemingly insurmountable odds, within us resides the strength not to be overpowered by the gusts of uncertainty but to glide in harmony with them. And on that inevitable day of departure, when we glance back to the day of arrival, we marvel at the vast distance we've traversed.

Credit: Technoblade

#Drip45

One Tree, One Life

\- August 05, 2023

My fervent love for the environment propelled me to take action, and on the 15th of July, with the help of my dedicated partner, I organized a transformative tree plantation drive at DAVV College, Indore, Madhya Pradesh, India. It filled me with joy to witness 20 like-minded individuals coming together to plant 50 trees, fostering a greener and healthier ecosystem. Through images and a Google Maps link, I proudly shared this accomplishment, hoping to inspire others to join the noble cause of preserving our planet for future generations.

Our Location: DAVV College

#Drip46

How Video Games Can and Should be Used for Education

- June 18, 2023

Video games are often seen as a waste of time, a distraction from learning, or a source of violence and addiction. However, I believe that video games and technology in general should be used more for education, because they can offer many benefits for students and teachers alike. Here are some reasons why:

- Video games can stimulate creativity and problem-solving skills. For example, Minecraft is a game where you can build anything you can imagine with blocks. You can create your own worlds, explore them, and share them with others. You can also learn about math, physics, and engineering by designing structures and mechanisms. Minecraft is like a digital Lego, but with infinite possibilities.

- Video games can also teach social and emotional skills. For example, Among Us is a game where you have to work together with your crewmates to find the impostor who is trying to sabotage the mission. You have to communicate effectively, trust your intuition, and deal with deception and betrayal. Among Us is like a virtual version of the classic party game Mafia, but with more fun and suspense.

- Video games can also make learning more fun and engaging. For example, Duolingo is an app that helps you learn a new language by playing games. You can earn points, level up, and compete with your friends. You can also choose from dozens of languages, from Spanish to Klingon. Duolingo is like a personal tutor, but with more gamification and motivation.

These are just some examples of how video games and technology in general can be used more for education. They can provide a rich and interactive learning environment that can cater to different learning styles and preferences. They can also make learning more enjoyable and rewarding, which can increase students' interest and retention. Therefore, I think that video games and technology in general should be used more for education, because they are not only fun, but also educational.

#Drip47

Genetic Engineering

- June 15, 2023

Genetic engineering is a great way to make the world a better place. Imagine being able to create new species of plants and animals that can help us solve some of the biggest problems we face. For example, we could engineer a super cow that produces more milk and less methane. That would be utterly amazing! Or we could engineer a super bee that pollinates more flowers, makes more honey, and doesn't sting. That would be beautiful! Or we could engineer a super human that is smarter, stronger, and healthier. That would be... wait, maybe that's not such a good idea. Let's not get ahead of ourselves.

Genetic engineering is not only beneficial to humanity, but to the world as a whole. It can help us fight diseases, improve crops, conserve biodiversity, and enhance our lives. Of course, it also comes with some risks and ethical issues, but nothing that we can't handle with some common sense and responsibility. After all, we are the ones who have the power to shape our own destiny. And with genetic engineering, we can do it in style. Just don't forget to read the fine print before you sign up for any experiments. You don't want to end up like Frankenstein's monster or Spider-Man's nemesis. Unless you're into that kind of thing.

#Drip48

The Apple Vision Pro

\- June 06, 2023

Today I want to share with you my feelings about the Apple Vision Pro, the latest and greatest AR/VR headset from our favorite fruit company. You may have seen the specs, the reviews, and the demos, and let me tell you, it's a roller coaster of emotions.

First of all, I feel excited. I mean, who wouldn't be excited about a device that can transform any room into your own personal theatre, let you interact with your apps in 3D space, and capture your memories in stunning spatial photos and videos? The Vision Pro promises to deliver a whole new level of immersive experiences that we've never seen before. It's like having a magic portal to another dimension on your face.

Secondly, I feel curious. I want to know more about how this device works, what it can do, and what it can't do. How does it track my eyes, hands, and voice? How does it blend digital content with my physical space? How does it adjust to different lighting conditions and environments? How does it handle battery life and overheating? How does it deal with privacy and security issues? There are so many questions that I want to ask Siri when I get my hands on one.

Lastly, I feel hopeful. Hopeful that Apple will continue to innovate and improve this technology and make it more accessible and affordable for everyone.

#Drip49

Quantum Computing

\- April 14, 2023

Quantum computing is said to be revolutionary, but what is it?

In a normal computer, like the one I am using to write this Drip, decisions are made using 1 or 0. For example, you click on a link. A signal is sent to tiny devices known as transistors, which decide where to go using 1 or 0. You can imagine 1 as yes, and 0 as no. After clicking on the link, a transistor is asked, 'open a new webpage?' 1 (yes). 'Show the user some personalized ads?' 0 (no).

I made this into a very simple function for your understanding, but actually, while clicking links, a lot of transistors are involved (Like at least 100,000).

On average, there are 3 billion transistors in a normal computer. You can increase the processing power of a computer by increasing the number of transistors it has. However, soon space runs out to put the transistors in the computer, so what do we do? Keep multiple options at one time. Yes and no. 0 and 1. This is known as superposition, being able to exist in 2 states or 2 places at the same time. Now the computer can make decisions even faster, increasing the processing power of the computer drastically.

For reference, a supercomputer can be a million times faster than the fastest laptop. A quantum computer is a 100 trillion times faster than the fastest supercomputer. Wow!

A quantum computer can do some calculations in 2 seconds, calculations which would take a supercomputer a long, long time (just until the time all of us are extinct).

One use of a quantum computer is that it is able to learn very fast, since it can process stuff faster than I can eat a burger. So, machine learning is a piece of cake for this computer.

So, quantum computers are a gift to humanity, right?

On the contrary, quantum computers can make hacking really easy. Remember how I said quantum computers can process stuff extremely fast? Well, people can use this to easily hack into anything within seconds. They just make a long list of possible passwords an account may have, and ask the computer to run through every single one of them, and since it can do it really fast, congratulations! It took 0.000065 seconds to find your password.

#Drip50

Myth vs Fact: We Only Use 10% of Our Brain

- February 21, 2023

Have you ever heard the claim that humans only use 10% of their brain? It's a popular myth that has been around for decades, but it's actually not true. In fact, we use all of our brain, all the time! Let's take a closer look at why this is just a myth.

Myth: We only use 10% of our brain.

Fact: We use all of our brain, all the time!

The 10% brain usage myth has been around for a long time, but it's simply not true. The idea that we only use a small part of our brain has been debunked by scientists and researchers who have studied the brain extensively.

The brain is a complex organ that controls all of our bodily functions, from our breathing to our thoughts and emotions. Every part of the brain is active and working all the time, even when we're sleeping.

It's true that certain parts of the brain are more active than others depending on what we're doing. For example, when we're reading, the part of our brain that processes language is more active. But that doesn't mean the rest of our brain is dormant.

In fact, studies have shown that even seemingly simple tasks like walking and talking require the use of multiple parts of the brain. So, it's clear that we use all of our brain, all the time.

So why does the 10% brain usage myth persist? It's possible that it's a result of a misunderstanding of brain imaging technology. Brain scans can show which parts of the brain are active during certain tasks, but they don't show how much of the brain is being used overall.

Additionally, the myth may have been perpetuated by popular culture, including movies and TV shows that portray characters with special abilities who are said to use more than 10% of their brain.

In conclusion, the idea that we only use 10% of our brain is just a myth. We use all of our brain, all the time, and every part of the brain is important for our bodily functions and cognitive processes. It's important to be skeptical of popular myths and to rely on scientific research and evidence to understand how our bodies and minds work.

#Drip51

Is World Peace Even a Remote Possibility?

- February 10, 2023

World peace seems like a dream that we all hope will come true, but the truth is, it's just not possible. There are lots of reasons why peace can never happen all over the world.

First of all, people are just too different from each other. Different countries have different ways of doing things and different beliefs. When these differences clash, it can lead to fighting and war. Just look at the conflict between Israel and Palestine, or the ongoing conflict in Syria, both are examples of how different beliefs and ways of life can lead to violence and war.

Another reason world peace is not possible is because some countries are just too powerful. They want to control other countries and make them do what they want. When other countries don't agree, it can lead to war. The United States is a great example of a powerful country that has tried to control other countries in the past.

Lastly, there is no one group or organization that has the power to make everyone follow the rules and keep the peace. The United Nations was created to try and keep peace, but it doesn't have enough power to make countries do what it wants.

#Drip52

Religious Freedom

- January 28, 2023

Practicing religion can be dangerous for a number of reasons. One of the main reasons is that it can lead to extremism and radicalization. When individuals become deeply invested in their religion, they may begin to view those who do not share their beliefs as inferior or even as enemies. This can lead to acts of violence and terrorism.

Another potential danger of practicing religion is that it can lead to social isolation and division. When individuals become too focused on their religious beliefs, they may begin to withdraw from society and become less engaged with the broader community. This can lead to a lack of understanding and empathy between different religious groups, which can further fuel extremism and conflict.

Additionally, some religious practices can be harmful to individuals themselves. For example, some religious groups may advocate for self-harm or other dangerous practices in the name of faith. In such cases, it is important for authorities to intervene to protect the well-being of these individuals.

Given these potential dangers, it is important for religious practices to be supervised and interfered with only in times of urgent need. This can help to ensure that religious beliefs and practices do not lead to extremism or harm to individuals or society.

#Drip53

Should Nuclear Energy be Used?

- January 26, 2023

Nuclear energy is a highly controversial topic, with many arguments both for and against its use. Those who oppose nuclear energy often cite the potential dangers of a nuclear accident or meltdown, as well as the long-term storage of nuclear waste. However, despite these concerns, there are several compelling reasons why nuclear energy should be used.

First and foremost, nuclear energy is a clean and efficient source of energy. Unlike fossil fuels, which produce harmful emissions and contribute to climate change, nuclear power plants produce virtually no greenhouse gases or air pollution. Additionally, nuclear energy is capable of producing large amounts of electricity with relatively small amounts of fuel. This makes it a highly efficient and cost-effective form of energy production.

Another key benefit of nuclear energy is its reliability. Nuclear power plants can operate continuously, 24 hours a day, seven days a week, providing a steady and dependable source of electricity. This is in contrast to renewable energy sources such as solar and wind power, which are dependent on weather conditions and can be unreliable.

It is also important to note that despite the public's perception of the dangers of nuclear energy, the history of nuclear energy has been relatively safe. The use of nuclear energy for power generation has resulted in very few accidents, and these accidents have resulted in relatively few deaths and injuries. Furthermore, the technology of nuclear power plants has come a long way since the early days of nuclear energy, and new safety features and design improvements have greatly reduced the risk of accidents.

Critics also point out the potential for nuclear weapons proliferation as a result of the development and spread of nuclear energy technology. However, it is important to note that the vast majority of countries that have developed nuclear energy for peaceful purposes have not used it to develop nuclear weapons. Additionally, international organizations such as the International Atomic Energy Agency (IAEA) work to monitor and prevent the spread of nuclear weapons.

#Drip54

Why Vaccines Should Be Mandatory

- January 10, 2023

Vaccines should be mandatory because they help protect not only the person who gets the vaccine, but also the people around them. For example, with the Covid-19 vaccine, not only does it protect the person who gets it from getting sick or dying from the virus, it also helps prevent the spread of the virus to others who might not be able to fight off the illness.

Another reason vaccines should be mandatory is because they have been proven to be safe and effective. Many people believe that vaccines can cause harm or have serious side effects, but this is just not true. The Covid-19 vaccine has been tested extensively and has been shown to be very safe with few side effects.

Furthermore, mandatory vaccines can help control and eliminate diseases. In the past, vaccines have been successful in eradicating diseases like smallpox and polio. If enough people get vaccinated, it creates herd immunity, which means that the disease can't spread easily and can eventually be eliminated. This is especially important for diseases that can be deadly or have severe consequences, like Covid-19.

Why The Death Penalty Should Be Abolished

- January 09, 2023

The death penalty is a controversial and divisive issue that has been debated for centuries. While some argue that it is necessary to deter crime and protect society, others believe that it is fundamentally wrong and should be abolished. I fall into the latter camp, and in this essay, I will explain why I believe that the death penalty is morally wrong and should be eliminated.

First and foremost, I believe that the death penalty is wrong because it violates the fundamental human right to life. Every person has the right to live, and it is not up to us or the government to decide when and how someone's life should end. This is especially true when we consider that there is always a risk of executing an innocent person. There have been numerous cases where individuals have been wrongly convicted and sentenced to death, only to be later exonerated by new evidence. In these cases, it is too late to correct the mistake, and an innocent person has lost their life because of a flawed system.

Additionally, I believe that the death penalty is not an effective deterrent to crime. Studies have shown that the threat of execution does not deter people from committing heinous crimes, and that other factors, such as poverty, mental illness, and access to education, play a much larger role in determining whether someone will commit a crime. Therefore, it is misguided to think that the death penalty will somehow solve the problem of crime and make our society safer.

Finally, I believe that the death penalty goes against the moral principles upheld by characters like Batman. Batman, a fictional character who is known for his dedication to justice and protection of the innocent, has a moral obligation to never take a life. In the Batman universe, he always seeks to find alternative solutions to problems and never resorts to killing his opponents. As a society, we should follow this example and strive to find ways to address crime and conflict that do not involve taking a life

#Drip56

Is Animal Cloning Ethical?

- January 08, 2023

Animal cloning is ethical because it can help to conserve species that are endangered or on the verge of extinction. With cloning, scientists are able to replicate the genetics of an animal and create a new individual with the same traits as the original. This can be especially useful for animals that are difficult to breed in captivity, or for those that have unique genetic traits that are important for the survival of their species.

Additionally, animal cloning can have a number of practical applications. For example, it can be used to produce genetically identical animals for use in research, which can help to reduce the number of animals that need to be used in scientific studies. It can also be used to produce animals with specific traits that are beneficial for farming or other industries, such as disease resistance or increased milk production.

Furthermore, animal cloning can be seen as a form of animal welfare, as it can help to prevent the suffering of animals that may be subjected to inhumane living conditions or treatment. By cloning animals that are well-cared for and living in good conditions, scientists can help to ensure that the animals being produced are also treated well and given the best possible chance at a good life.

In conclusion, animal cloning is ethical because it has the potential to conserve endangered species, has practical applications, and can be seen as a form of animal welfare. While there may be some concerns about the ethics of cloning, these can be addressed through careful regulation and oversight to ensure that the animals being cloned are treated ethically and with respect.

#Drip57

Should Kids Have Cell Phones?

- December 21, 2022

In this Drip, "kids" are children below the age of 13.

I have been using a cellphone since I was 12. However, this was a necessity. Since Covid had struck, everything had been shifted online, including school. The main work of our school was being done on WhatsApp, which only works on phones. I couldn't keep borrowing my mom's phone while she was working, so I was given a phone.

Phones can have very harmful effects on kids. I have seen 13-year-olds spend several hours on the phone. The primary time consumer was, of course, the one, the only (drumroll please) Instagram. Now, I'm not going to talk about social media here. However, social media is a big part of a smartphone.

Although, if a kid is in some emergency, they should have a way of contacting emergency services or their parents/guardians. To solve this dilemma, kids should be given a non-smartphone. This will definitely lower their time on a phone and be available to use during urgent situations.

#Drip58

Humans are No Different

- November 25, 2022

Humans keep comparing others to animals. “Hey, dude! You eat like an animal!” But aren’t we animals ourselves? We have evolved from apes. That is common knowledge. However, many, many humans fail to see that we are still apes. No matter the evolution. We still have their palms, hair in all the same places but less in size and number, and we are still four-limbed. The only difference is that they eat fruits, and I don’t.

We are all one species right now, called Homo sapiens, but it wasn’t always like that. There used to be a lot of other species, but the most prominent ones at one point were Neanderthals. Neanderthals were big and muscular, kind of like NFL players. They didn’t have a brain as big as Sapiens, but they made up for it in strength. How, then, did Sapiens survive? It was language. Language is the best gift ever given to man. Without language, we would not be alive right now. With language, people were able to communicate. They could signal to each other if a threat were approaching, but even other animals could do that. Sapiens could tell where the predator was, where it was going if it was in a pack or not, or even its Instagram ID.

Obviously, Sapiens were superior to Neanderthals, but without one gift, without one tiny part of the brain, without the best stroke of luck anyone will ever have, we would have been punier than chimpanzees, gorillas, or monkeys. If Gorillas got language, they would easily wipe out humans. Take Gorrila Grod from DC comics. We should not think of ourselves as above them or more sophisticated than them, because things like jobs or social status don't matter to them; just that their belly stays full. In the vast world, the other animals only care about survival; as you can see, elephants are surviving, and so are sloths.

#Drip59

NFTs: The Good and The Bad

- November 08, 2022

A few months ago, NFTs were blowing up like crazy. Everybody wanted to invest in them, and it was the main talk for tech enthusiasts for months. They are handy and exciting but have quite a few drawbacks.

First of all, what is an NFT? NFT stands for 'Non-Fungible Token.' Fungible means something that can be exchanged or replaced for the same value or divided into smaller pieces that add up to the same value. Some examples of fungible tokens are dollars or bitcoin. NFTs are the complete opposite of these. Every single NFT is unique. It is rare. NFTs use blockchain to ensure who owns the NFT.

This has several advantages. If a person made digital art or videos and released them to the public instantly, they would lose all ownership over that product. This can be done by simple screenshotting or screen recording. But if the person releases it as an NFT, they would have complete ownership over that product. It doesn't matter if someone screenshots it; the blockchain technology of NFTs will ensure that the person owns it. NFTs can also motivate video game players to play the game more by rewarding them with one-of-a-kind

NFTs to which no one else has access. This will allow the players to earn money by playing these games, getting the NFT, and then selling the NFT.

Among these pros, however, lie several cons. First and foremost, if you buy an NFT of, let's say, a custom-made superhero, you don't get any rights to it. You can't make a movie, T.V. show, or any merch of that superhero. You're not the owner. You have ownership over that NFT. Possessing an NFT is just a little more than bragging rights. Another problem is that these art pieces that are being made are not made by an artist who really put their heart into their painting. Many of these are just made by people in business for cash grabs.

What do you think? Are NFTs helping people, or are they just another way for people to make easy cash?

Should Sports be Compulsory in School?

- November 07, 2022

Sports are a significant aspect of life. Although they are necessary to learn essential life skills, some students may argue that they are wasting their time and that they should spend that time doing academics or something they want to build a future out of. I disagree with these students but to a certain extent.

Sports help a student to know what it is like to be a part of a team. Teamwork can be done in a classroom, but how you get to know someone when your body is full of adrenaline cannot be compared. Sports also help students get a certain sense of discipline, which is impossible in academics. Physical exercise can also tire a person, resulting in a night of better and sounder sleep. Physical activity can also help prevent major diseases like diabetes, hypertension, heart disease, and even certain types of cancer.

Having said this, sports are only sometimes suitable for students. Injuries, ranging from a simple toe twist to a devastating ligament tear, have a higher probability of happening while doing sports rather than sitting in a classroom. Some competitive sports can lead to a person being disappointed or even humiliated if they lose, which is not very good for mental health. It can be expensive since you have to pay to get equipment and to get into some tournaments. Sports are also very time-consuming, and if sports are compulsory, then the students who want to be better at academics or want to pursue something else in life are just wasting their time.

One of the solutions for this is that sports should be compulsory, but to and from a certain age. Students who start a particular sport early have more time to build a good foundation. However, this isn't without drawbacks since even a minor injury could be nasty for a small kid. Sports should not be compulsory after grade 9; in grade 10, some students have a vague idea of what they want to do, and the academics get tougher. Those who don't can still attend sports if they want to, but those who do will waste their time.

#Drip61

How Free Should Speech Be?

- October 26, 2022

In almost every democratic country, the right to freedom of speech is exercised. This is an essential pillar of democracy; without it, a nation is not fit to call itself democratic. But a lot of the time, this could lead to the endangering of public safety. So how free should speech be?

The government should interfere only when it is vital and involves public safety, no other reason. The problem here is how does a person define ‘necessary’? Who’s going to be the judge? If something involves public safety, law enforcement does not have time to go to court and get a warrant. I think this is where someone with high authority should step in. They can make the decision of whether to let the news go public or not. Still, the fact that the authority stepped in and stopped the information from being released should become public after the particular event occurs.

This approach could be better and has several flaws in it. One is that if the news could have saved some lives or wouldn’t have affected public safety, it can’t be changed. The deed is already done. Another is that the person could use this power for their own benefit and not think about the nation. No approach is perfect, but I believe that this is the best course of action.

#Drip62

Should We Invest Money in Outer Space

- October 25, 2022

Currently, space corporations and governments are heavily investing in outer space. But is it worth looking to the stars when we have our own problems to deal with?

First of all, NASA does not spend nearly as much on space as you think. A public survey states that most people think NASA takes up about a quarter of the US budget. In reality, however, NASA takes up only 0.3% of the USA's federal budget!

Oh, and that memory foam bed that you sleep on? It was made by NASA researchers looking for ways to cushion the pilot. Another thing that we use in our everyday lives is influenced directly by space: GPS/Google Maps. Without satellites orbiting the Earth, people would have great difficulty finding a route to a place.

When the Earth inevitably dies, we will need another place to stay. This other place is going to be another planet. I love the Earth as much as the next person, but we must think ahead.

The more we look to the skies, the more we learn about our planet. We can compare it with other worlds we see and try to improve the things which have a problem.

"The Earth is the cradle of humanity, but mankind cannot stay in the cradle forever."- Konstantin Tsiolkovsky.

#Drip63

Homework Should be Banned

- October 24, 2022

You may think that this Drip is biased. I am a student, and I can assure you that no student in history has ever liked homework. But I will try my best to be as impartial as possible.

Homework should be banned. After school, a student's last desire is to go back home and study again. The student may wish to explore something outside of school studies, like programming or art. If there is homework, the student either doesn't have time to do it or is too tired to do anything else.

A person might argue what schools should do about the leftover work. Well, the school should try to complete it in the allocated time. If that is not possible, do it the next day in school. Increase the time that a period takes and decrease another one which is not as far behind in the course as the previous one.

Again, there are some benefits of homework as well. The load on the teacher decreases as they do not have to do everything in a single period. The time the teacher has with the students can be used to teach the students something, and the menial work, like copying something in your notebook, can be done at home.

It all depends on the teacher's teaching speed and the student's learning pace.

#Drip64

Should Students be Allowed to Choose Their Own Subjects?

- October 23, 2022

One of the most annoying things I find about school is that I have to study subjects in which I am not interested. A few examples come to mind: history, geography, biology, and my second language, French. It doesn't mean that these are bad subjects, just that they don't appeal to me or won't be helpful later in my work. Suppose I have already decided what I want to study later on. In that case, I am simply wasting my time studying other subjects. Of course, schools should teach these subjects to all the students up to a specific grade. Kids also need time to figure out what they want to do. In my opinion, the subjects students don't want to study should be taught up to grade 10 (like it is now). Still, the student gets to choose what subjects they want to give in the qualifying exams like the boards. If I give a French board exam and do not get good marks, my overall score goes down even though I never wanted to take French in the first place!

In conclusion, students should only give exams in subjects they want to learn or make a career out of only after grade 9.

#Drip65

Religion Through a Teenager's Perspective

- October 20, 2022

I am an atheist, but I appreciate people who believe in God. They have something to hold on to during hard times, or someone you can have faith in whenever you want. The thing that I find really annoying, however, is people turning to God only during hard times. Or how people believe in God only when they want something they really desire.

My family is Jain. Jains have a special ritual in their temples where they give the idol of any God a bath. I once went to witness this. I came back with zero respect for the people who were doing it. There was one main guy who I assumed was the 'owner' of the temple. A lot of people were there who wanted to do this. So, the 'owner' started auctioning who gets to do this! And it wasn't like the money was going to go to an orphanage or anything. It was going into the guy's own pocket. He had turned religion into profit! And the people were willing to pay about three thousand dollars just to do this!

This is only one instance of religion being turned into profit. There is even a whole movie about it. I also don't like the divisions religion creates. The best example of this is when India and Pakistan separated. Muslims went one side, and Hindus went another. This shouldn't have happened just because one side believes in one type of God and the other believes in some other type of God.

In conclusion, religion is good as long as you don't take it too far. As long as you stay sincere and not use it to manipulate other people for your own interests. As long as you're faithful.

Vegetarianism

- October 16, 2022

Vegetarianism is a big part of my life. My whole family is vegetarian, and I myself do not eat "non-veg" food. But I have never understood why. Why do some people prefer not to eat animals? The reason I get the most is that animals move. We can see animals hurt when they die. That is why we do not eat animals. But don't plants also feel pain?

Scientists have concluded that plants do indeed have a nervous system. They can also feel pain but in a way animals can't comprehend. So, what is the difference between eating a plant and an animal? I think that people (including me) often do not eat animals because they find it repulsive. Gruesome. Disgusting.

That's not to say that being a non-vegetarian is good. A major contribution to the global warming issue is that cows in a factory that makes beef produce a lot of methane (farts). If everyone in the whole world went vegetarian right now, food related emissions would drop by 60%. SIXTY PERCENT! This is one of the reasons why I have decided to stay vegetarian.

#Drip67

An Apple Obsession

- October 14, 2022

Apple. One of the most successful companies in the world. For me, it is beautiful because of its simplicity. The way just put the number of things necessary into anything: Their software, stock apps, or products like the iPhone. Whenever I use Android or Windows, I find unnecessary things in the way, like the number of apps on the right side of the Windows search bar, or the extra number of features that almost no one ever uses in Microsoft Word.

Apple is not all good though. Some of their products are too expensive (cough Air Pods Max cough). I myself find a lot of bugs in the MacOS software which make the whole experience very irritating. The lack of compatibility is also very frustrating. Games I would really like to play are not on the Mac since not a lot of people buy a Mac to play video games. After the recent shift to Apple Silicon, even more apps are not working due to the different build of the chip. Whatever the cons though, this company will always be the Apple of my eyes.

#Drip68

My Room, My Universe

- October 13, 2022

There is something special about my room. It's not very commodious, but it still feels like I've got enough room to put another house in here. Everything is just so neatly arranged. My study table, the charging port below my study table that has just enough ports to support my devices, my secret place where I stash all of my junk food, and of course, my brilliant and comfy bed.

When I lie down on my bed, it feels like I'll just sink into it. Sink into it, and keep falling, and falling, until eventually, I wake up. That is the big disadvantage of it. Waking up feels like torture every morning. The bed is soooooo comfortable that I never want to leave it. It's the reason why I've grown to hate waking up early.

During Covid-19, I spent twenty out of twenty-four hours holed up in here. There were four things I did during those times: Study, eat, play, and sleep. Honestly, nothing can compare to this heavenly abode. The only thing I need now is a mini fridge to store my drinks and BAM! You'll never see me out of that room again!

#Drip69

What is Right?

- April 02, 2025

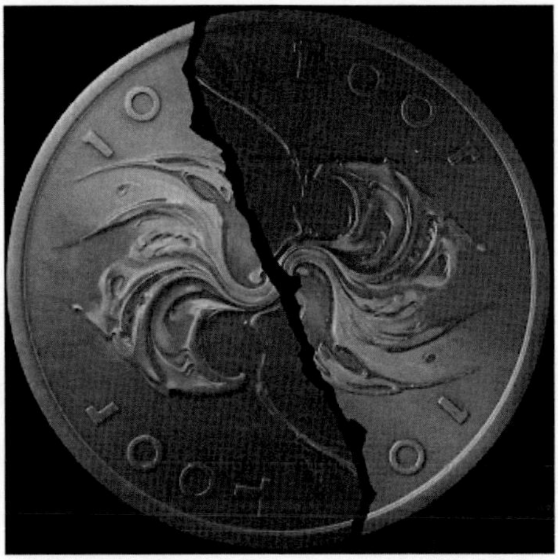

The way we humans decide what is right and what is wrong will always depend on what the majority of the population thinks. Always.

Let's take an example. Around the 15th century in Europe, a type of medicine was extremely prevalent: corpse medicine. It was widely believed that consuming parts of the human body (think powdered skulls) could cure things like ailments and pains. It wasn't just believed either; it was socially acceptable. Right now, anybody you ask would be disgusted by it, "How could they even think of doing that?"

Because throughout history we can see that ideas and morals have evolved. Not improved. Evolved. Why do I say that?

Instead of the past, let's jump to the future. With veganism spreading farther and wider, it is safe to assume that maybe in 50–100 years, maybe even in our lifetimes, it won't be "right" to eat, let's say, chicken. You can't kill one, you can't eat one. Those people in the future will look at their history books and think that we were morally wrong, the same way we look back at corpse medicine. Does it mean we are wrong? No. In our time, a majority of people believe that chickens provide good protein, taste amazing, whatever. Right now, 99% of the people you ask will say that yes, it is wrong to consume human remains. Does it mean that the 15th century Europeans were wrong? No. A majority of the people in their time thought it was acceptable to treat illness using skulls, so they were, in a way, right.

Another example is dowry in India. Even 40 years ago it was prevalent and was a major reason for harassment and humiliation of women and their families. Back then, it was still practiced widely, and in many places, socially expected. Today, the majority sees it as deeply problematic, even criminal. Has morality improved? Or has it just changed with the tide of time and awareness?

So why did I say that ideas and morals have not improved? Because our set of morals and ideas are just another era in this perpetual spiral of beliefs. Saying that we are the only ones who are correct is an arrogant way to live, don't you think?

Acknowledgements

I am deeply grateful to Murugu Uncle (Mr. M. M. Murugappan), who has been a mentor and wise soundboard through what I like to call my journey. His patience, insight, and ability to bridge the generational gap so smoothly has turned an interaction which most people would consider formal into something which I consider a genuine friendship. His belief in me and genuine interest in listening gives me the confidence to grow: not just as a writer, but as a teenager trying to figure things out. To walk alongside someone who has these abilities makes me feel very lucky.

To my mother, who, let's be honest, didn't suggest but more like *gently imposed* the idea of writing: thank you. Thank you for your unwavering encouragement. Your belief in my (whining) voice and your unconditional love have proven you've always been my loudest cheerleader (quite literally), and the kind of mother whose strength, warmth, and humor make everything feel possible. You've not only cared about my dreams, but also reminded me time and again of the importance of staying grounded and true to myself.

To Dada, my brother, the robin to my batman, and the Kyrie to my LeBron, thank you for being the best sibling anyone could hope for. You're always present and always able to make me lighter. I didn't realize growing up, but your presence is the best gift ever.